LESSONS FROM A
Troubadour

"*Lessons from a Troubadour* offers a rich exploration of the breadth and depth of Catholic spiritual tradition. John Michael Talbot, sharing from his own conversion story and the sources of inspiration for his music and preaching, helps us see how Catholic spirituality can shape the daily lives of people who seek to follow Jesus more closely."

Cardinal Donald Wuerl
Archbishop of Washington

"John Michael Talbot is one of Christian music's most well-known artists, and a man who has given everything he has to follow Jesus the Lord. Though he has written nearly forty books, *Lessons from a Troubadour* stands out from all the rest. Almost journal-like, these parables, prose, and stories are folksy, deep, revelatory, and vetted from millions of miles of road ministry. I have toured with John Michael, shared meals, and asked him many questions about life, faith, and music. But now I know he was holding back! From the crazy pancake breakfast that inspired the magnificent song "Holy Is His Name," to his thoughts on the landmark recordings *The Lord's Supper* and *The Painter*, this book is almost a spiritual tell-all. Yet the final section moves way beyond music and theological reflection as John Michael opens his heart in a deep and personal way and offers both his successes and perceived failings as a source of inspiration and challenge for those who want to follow Jesus into deeper waters of faith."

Tom Booth
Composer and artist, speaker, retreat leader, and spiritual director

"To understand theological truths is great, but to see theological truths in everyday life is transforming. When the mundane becomes an adventure, you know that God is with you. You will be inspired by John Michael's observations and insights as he has not only been walking with the Lord for a long time, but also seeing things we often miss."

Jeff Cavins
Founder of The Great Adventure Bible Study

"Meditate on these pages and you'll learn where the beautiful songs came from. They came from a full life—John Michael Talbot's—and they came from the spiritual realities he's pursued with a singular passion. His melodies have been with me for decades. These pages have the same staying power."

Mike Aquilina
Author of *A History of the Church in 100 Objects*

"Almost every morning on the way to work, I listen to John Michael Talbot. He is one of the great Catholic voices of our times—not just as a musician but also through his speeches and writings. I highly encourage you to seek him out and engage him to inspire your parish or group."

Matthew Kelly
Founder of Dynamic Catholic

"John Michael Talbot has put his deep love for the Lord and his extraordinary musical talent at the service of the Church. His dedication to Christ will be an inspiration to all who hear him."

Most Rev. Peter Sartain
Archbishop of Seattle

"I believe that in years to come, John Michael Talbot will be remembered alongside those such as Thomas Merton as one who brought the richest and most significant attention to modern monastic life and the spirituality of the hermitage."

Tom Cordero
Director of music for the Diocese of Brooklyn

"John Michael Talbot shares his spiritual path with the special touch of a musician. In *Lessons from a Troubadour*, readers' hearts will sing as they participate in his rich experiences and learn the basics of the Christian spiritual life. Here, John Michael enriches and inspires us to search for God in our own lives, to find that God is present in many ways, and to realize that we must just be open to discover his love for us."

Abbot Primate Emeritus Notker Wolf, O.S.B.
Guitarist with the Christian rock band Feedback

LESSONS FROM A
Troubadour

A

Lifetime

of

Parables,

Prose,

and

Stories

John Michael Talbot

AVE MARIA PRESS AVE Notre Dame, Indiana

© 2018 by John Michael Talbot

All rights reserved. No part of this book may be used or reproduced in any manner whatsoever, except in the case of reprints in the context of reviews, without written permission from Ave Maria Press®, Inc., P.O. Box 428, Notre Dame, IN 46556, 1-800-282-1865.

Founded in 1865, Ave Maria Press is a ministry of the United States Province of Holy Cross.

www.avemariapress.com

Paperback: ISBN-13 978-1-59471-845-8

E-book: ISBN-13 978-1-59471-846-5

Cover and text design by Katherine Robinson.

Printed and bound in the United States of America.

Library of Congress Cataloging-in-Publication Data

Names: Talbot, John Michael, author.

Title: Lessons from a troubadour : a lifetime of parables, prose, and stories / John Michael Talbot.

Description: Notre Dame, Indiana : Ave Maria Press, [2018]

Identifiers: LCCN 2018018963 (print) | LCCN 2018025766 (ebook) | ISBN 9781594718465 (ebook) | ISBN 9781594718458 (pbk.)

Subjects: LCSH: Talbot, John Michael. | Composers--United States--Biography. | Christian life.

Classification: LCC ML410.T139 (ebook) | LCC ML410.T139 A3 2018 (print) | DDC

782.42164092--dc23

LC record available at https://lccn.loc.gov/2018018963

Contents

PART THREE: The Church

PART FOUR: The Future Lies before Us

Introduction

It seems like a lifetime has already gone by, but I believe there is still some time left before me.

I began as a musician who achieved some success in a country rock group in the late 1960s and early '70s. I first accepted Christ in the Jesus Movement of that time, after desperately searching through world religions for a spiritual answer to the questions our countercultural movement was so earnestly asking. My music grew through many concerts and recordings in the first generation of contemporary Christian music. After seven years I found a deeper answer in the monastic and Franciscan expressions of Catholic Christianity. I found beauty in mystery and balanced fullness.

My music continued and became more successful than I ever expected or imagined. I also founded a new integrated monastic community. I immersed myself in patristics from the orthodox Catholic tradition and the teachings of the contemplatives, mystics, and monastic Fathers and Mothers. I taught what I encountered. This tradition is radical, practical, and mystical all at once. It defies labels such as *conservative* or *progressive*. I shared some of that wisdom between songs in concerts, some in retreats, and some in parish missions and diocesan conventions.

For decades I have condensed that teaching into short parables, prose-like paradoxes, analogies, and stories worth telling. I have titled books with them and used them in books to illustrate points. I have drawn from them in retreats and parish ministries. I have also used these teachings in my larger concerts.

Over the years, many people have requested a compilation. This book is an attempt to meet that request. It is not a systematic work of any kind; it is not what anyone would or should call *theology*. I have written those sorts of books before. Instead, this book is a collection of prose and parables—my way of explaining some of the basics of faith in ordinary language, if you will.

Parables and prose can sing without being songs. They can teach without feeling like teachings. Prose is a natural flow of speech without the structures of poetry yet with some of its beauty and brevity. It is not mere street talk, nor is it scholarly writing. It is a simpler song in speech. Parables draw comparisons between special spiritual or moral teachings and things that we know in ordinary life. A parable often compares the extraordinary with the ordinary. It makes the extraordinary approachable to the average person. It says more by saying less.

Though parables and stories are short, we can return to them again and again throughout our lives to find a deeper meaning and application. They reach the simple and the wise, the learned and the unlearned. They break down barriers between people. I believe that is why Jesus taught with parables instead of theology. No doubt, he knew both. But he used parables to reach everyone. He quoted nature and humanity as easily as he quoted scripture. My little parables have none of the greatness of the ones Jesus used, but his remain my source and inspiration.

Parables are both mystical and practical. They are easily understood by the common worker and remain deeply challenging to the greatest mystic and theologian. Jesus attracted common people more than theologians and religious leaders, but he got their attention. He first impressed the theologians and religious authorities through parables. But they were also offended once they felt too challenged by them. Parables can be both approachable and puzzling. What we do with them makes all the difference.

I pray that you will enjoy these paradoxical teachings of holy and ordinary matters. I hope that these teachings reveal what life is all about for you, as they have for me. And I hope the little stories you read here will humanize the teachings a bit. Pray them. For every word and idea in this collection there are shelves of books of scripture, patristics, and mystical works you might explore further. Maybe intersperse reading them with some of my music or that of other favorite contemplative or meditative artists.

Do not read this like a book of theology, but rather let your theology be enriched by what you read here. Let it touch you prayerfully and mystically. Then allow it to enrich your daily life in Christ and the Church. That would be a great gift to me. It would make writing my thoughts down worthwhile.

PART ONE

Holy God

The Voice, the Eternal, the Music

My earliest memories of God are from when I was around five years old. I remember playing outside, and often pausing to think about who or what created the water in our pond, the trees in our yard, or even the breezes that blew through the Oklahoma plains. I felt God's gentle but profound touch in those times. But who or what touched me remained a mystery.

I didn't much like church. I didn't like dressing up in uncomfortable clothes to worship God, but I loved the music and good preaching. Later, I came to know God personally as Jesus; I began to pray and study Catholic Christianity as well as the religions of the world to find more sophisticated experiences and explanations.

God is the Voice that calls us to the Word in and beyond all words.

God is the Being that gives meaning to every being yet is above our comprehension of being.

God is the Eternal that calls us to eternity from and in time.

He is the Infinite that calls us to infinity in and beyond space.

God is the Music that calls us to the sound that can be seen and the color that can be heard.

He is the Artist who calls us to an artwork that gives meaning to yet is beyond all earthly art.

Are we really hearing and listening to his voice today?

Paradox, Mystery, and Balance

God is Mystery. This Mystery is clearly revealed in paradox and balance.

A paradox is an apparent contradiction that speaks a deeper truth. Some paradoxes:

- We often find companionship, communion, and community in solitude.
- We often hear God's Word best in silence.
- We find spiritual wealth in simplicity and poverty.
- We discover freedom in obedience to God and to his experienced teachers on earth.
- We find pure companionship in celibacy and chastity.

We then go on to find such paradoxes as these:

- Glory in humility and even in humiliation
- Peace in the midst of conflict
- Joy in sorrow
- Consolation in desolation
- Life in death

These paradoxes all speak a deeper truth that can be understood on the deepest level by people searching for spiritual awakening in their lives. Paradoxes can open the doorway from the old, unhappy self to a new self, fulfilled in the Spirit of God.

These paradoxes are mysteries and cannot be comprehended by natural reason alone. They have a logic that defies mere human logic. To seek to understand such mysteries implies that one is opening up to the mystical, that which cannot be understood by logic alone.

But once we glimpse these paradoxes and mysteries, even from a distance, we see that all things proclaim a logic more complete and balanced than anything the world has ever known.

This is the source and goal of all religion and spirituality.

Religion is a yoke we willingly embrace to ultimately set us free. As Jesus says, "For my yoke is easy, and my burden light" (Mt 11:30). As the wisdom literature teaches, wisdom is like a weighty yoke under which we willingly stoop our shoulders when we are young so that she may support us when we are feeble and old.

So there is a balance between doctrine and mysticism. And there is a beauty in that balance.

We begin with orthodox teaching regarding faith and morality. What or who is God, and how does he want us to live? How do we live as his united people? These things are basic.

We then move on to deeper and higher things. We move on to Mystery.

It's like playing a guitar. I was always inspired by good music. It sparked something mystical and beautiful in my heart and soul. But in order to make good music, I had to embrace the discipline of long hours of study and practice. I practiced until my fingers bled. The mystical spark of the beauty of music inspired me to keep at it and keep on. Only after much study and practice, and copying other people's styles and songs, did my own style, sound, and song emerge.

The same thing is true of paradoxes, mysteries, and balance. We must find the balance between doctrine and mysticism, the mind and the heart, the known and the unknown, to find the beauty of God.

Both Beyond and Personal

God is a name we give to the One above all names. The Hebrews called him *YHWH*, or "the One beyond all comprehension or naming"; and *Elohim*, or "the One we can know" as both plural and neuter. The Greeks called him *Theos*. We call him God.

God is the Force behind all that is. He is the Force in every and beyond all force. But God is not merely a force.

God is also personal. He is *hypostasis*. He is not merely a *prosopon* (Greek, meaning "face" or "mask"), nor is he mere *physis* (Greek for "nature"). God is the Person. All persons flow from him and find their true personhood only in him.

God is good. Goodness must flow out to another. Yet God is One, so to whom does he flow? Must God create in order to have another to receive his goodness? No. That would reduce him to being merely a god, not God. He must flow out to Another *within the One* in order to be God. God must be plural and one. This is a paradox, but it remains a deeper truth. It both completes and is beyond logic.

Do we cling to a mere human and earthbound logic, or do we allow God to reveal a more perfect logic found in paradox?

One ties us to earth. The other launches us into eternity in the here and now.

Creation and the Creator

God is beyond space and time. He is infinite and omnipresent, or present everywhere in space and time, in infinity and eternity, all at once.

Creation bears God's traces. The Creator also works in and through creation. Jesus is the incarnation of God in space and time—God-with-us. But we also believe in the resurrection of the body, and in a real heaven and hell. This is far beyond what we can now comprehend. But we've glimpsed it already in science.

Most believe that we live in three dimensions; four, if we count time. But quantum physics now theorizes that there are at least twelve to sixteen potential dimensions. There could be even more. What are the other eight to twelve? We can only guess, but the ideas are myriad and mind boggling. The universe is multidimensional, and this is only the physical universe.

The Eastern Christian Fathers tell us that the human spirit has the capacity to intuit infinity and eternity in the here and now of space and time even though they are beyond our full intellectual, emotional, or sensual ability to grasp. When we are reborn by the Spirit of God, the human spirit inside us is reborn and awakened. It then becomes the primary faculty that is processed through our minds, emotions, and senses. We gain the capacity to glimpse both created and uncreated multidimensional reality.

Jesus exemplifies this most perfectly as Son of God and Son of Man. After his resurrection, Jesus can appear as himself or as someone else. He has physicality but can walk into a room without coming through the door or even the window.

The heavenly Jerusalem has physical streets of gold that are something we can relate to. But those streets are also transparent and beyond what we can relate to in our physical universe.

Our new life in Christ means that we share in his resurrection beginning here on earth and reaching its fullness in heaven. This is what we are made for, and where we are ultimately headed. Heaven is creation in its fullness, for it is in full communion with God the Creator. Heaven is the fullness of Creator and creation, the spiritual and the phenomenal.

We are made for a physical universe that is beyond the limited one we currently inhabit. We are transformed and completed through the grace of the Spirit in our spirits. "What eye has not seen, and ear has not heard, and what has not entered the human heart, what God has prepared for those who love him" (1 Cor 2:9). Yet when we experience it fully, we will know what we were made for, and that for which we inherently long.

Are we ready?

God's Love and Our Freedom

God pours out his goodness and love in creation. He does not need to, but he wants to and does so freely. Creation only finds its fulfillment in the Creator. All creation bears his traces.

God freely created human beings in his image and likeness. We are spirit, soul, and body—tripartite as a reflection of his Trinity. Like the smooth surface of a still pond, our humanity reflects divinity in a completely unique way on earth. When we sinned, we lost God's likeness but still bear his image. We were turned upside down when we made the body primary and covered the spirit and soul as if in deep slumber. Our pond is agitated but still reflects his image, albeit a fractured and broken one. We still hunger for him in our desire for truth, beauty, and love.

God sends no one to hell; we must choose that for ourselves. To go to hell is an obstinate insistence to live independently of God. Why would anyone choose to live apart from perfect goodness and love? That is called the "mystery of iniquity."

When creation departed through sin from full communion with God, it got off the path. "Off the path" is the meaning of *hamartia*, the primary Greek word for *sin*. We got lost in the desert and wilderness, all tangled up in the weeds of life, and could not find the Promised Land. Yet we continue to long for God because we are created in his image. We long for truth, beauty, goodness, and love, but cannot find it by our own power alone. We need God's help to get back on the path.

This is a natural revelation in the philosophies and religions of the world. The truth contained in them comes from

God and leads us back to God. But they are not perfect revelation. When used wrongly, they can lead us away from God.

God sent us the Law and the prophets through the
Chosen People as extraordinary or supernatural revelation.
From the burning bush on Sinai, to the Temple, to prophetic
schools of the Judean and Galilean hills, God prepared a
way for his full revelation. When all this was written in the
Jewish scriptures, it was as though God sent us a "letter" to
prepare us for his full personal visit among us.

God sent us his Son as that full revelation. In him he
paid us a personal visit. All revelation before him, both natural and supernatural, pointed to him and finds its completion
only in him. God's Son, incarnated on earth, has a name.
That name is Jesus. It is his name for all eternity.

Jesus dies out of love so all might live in his love.

God is our Father, who heals all fathers, mothers, and
children from the fear and anger of abuse and from misun-
derstanding in broken families and homes. God the Father
sends his Son, who heals broken relationships with brothers
and sisters. God is the Spirit, who empowers us with an
enthusiasm that brings the Father and the Son to us as a
life-changing personal experience. Individuals and communities can then know God beyond a mere idea or theology.
Each is in all, and all is in each, yet without confusion.

Jesus reveals all of this—and more—beyond our limited
understanding or words.

Meeting Jesus

My first memories of Jesus are from Methodist Sunday school, when I was five or six years old. A simple picture of Jesus the Good Shepherd on the wall in my classroom touched me deeply, and has stayed with me until this day. I did not know him yet, but I was strongly attracted to him.

I began to meet Jesus later when Jesus Freaks met me in airports, or lay evangelists came to my front door, or even when a Billy Graham crusade was on TV. Sometimes I was put off by their crudeness. Sometimes, somehow, I was attracted. My interest was piqued.

So I searched through volumes of scripture and writings about Jesus. Some were Christian, and some were from other religions. Some were Protestant, and some were Catholic. I was profoundly attracted to the great teacher, mystic, and prophet—Jesus.

It would only be later that I would have a full personal encounter with Jesus, one that would change me forever.

Who is Jesus? This is a question that haunted the religious leaders of his day, and even his followers when he walked the earth. It remained a burning question in the developing Christology of the Early Church and in the patristic era. It remains a perennial question for us today. I do not presume to provide an adequate answer. But I offer these few reflections.

For me, Jesus is the Teacher of teachers. He is the King of kings, and the Lord of lords. He is the Mystic of mystics, and Prophet of prophets.

For the Jews he was the promised son of David; he was the King of kings and Lord of lords, the Messiah.

For Romans he was more than a son of a god; he was *the* Savior, the *only* Son of the *One True* God.

For other religions he might well be called the Master of masters, the Guru of gurus, the Sage of sages, and the Enlightened One of enlightened ones. But these are outside the scope of scripture, which arose from the Jews and in the West.

But all such titles only point to a Reality beyond our full comprehension or the grasp of the human intellect. Yet the titles remain true.

Jesus Is God and Man

Christians say that Jesus is God and he is man. That is more than we can understand, and even that falls short. Jesus is fully man and fully God. He is weakness and strength, and strength in weakness. He is vulnerable and invulnerable, and invulnerable in vulnerability. Jesus is the Almighty in the powerless babe in the manger, the All-Knowing with finite human understanding, and the Ever-Present in a limited human body. He is the beauty of both without losing the fullness of either. He shares in our humanity so that we might share in his divinity.

Jesus is the Paradox of paradoxes. A paradox is an apparent contradiction that speaks a deeper truth. He is mystery and clear manifestation. He comforts and confounds. He clarifies with divine knowledge and confuses on the mere human level. But he is not untrue. Jesus is the Truth. All genuine truth leads back to God. When partial or used wrongly, it can lead us away from God. God is the author of all truth.

The devil is the father of lies and can only pervert truth. He is the original gossip and slanderer. He is a fallen angel. He leads away from God by misusing the things of God. Yet the devil is not the dark side of God; he is a mere creature of God, an angel of a very high order who turned away from his Creator. He has no capacity to create. He can only distort creation and pervert truth with half-truths. Jesus, however, is fully true. He is the Creator, the One through whom everything is made. The devil's promises are alluring in the short term, but they are untrue in the long run and in the eternal. Trusting them, many have followed the wrong way.

Jesus simply *is*. Earthly truth can only point to such Truth. Earthly thoughts, ideas, or imaginations only point to him. He complements and completes them. He also surpasses them all. Jesus also complements and completes all religions. He confirms the truth in all religion by surpassing religion and establishing a new religion that is fully Spirit filled.

Jesus is the Way. He is the Path. He comes from God and leads back to God. His path is sure and true. All others are incomplete or fall short, though their words and teachings may be eloquent and beautiful. Remember that to sin simply means to get off the path. Despite our inherent divine desire to go the right direction, sin leads us off the path to our Destination. Jesus is the Way that leads us out of the weeds of wilderness and back to God.

Jesus is the Life. His life shows us the way to live by living among us. As Paradox of paradoxes, his life is revealed most clearly in his death, and his death leads to resurrection and even greater life.

Most of us have settled for a version of ourselves that is less than we were really created to be. We have settled for an "us" that is not really "us." Jesus empowers us to rediscover who we were really created to be. Jesus shows us how to be human and enables us to become more fully human by sharing in his divine gift. He shows us how to be fully human by being more than human. And he shows us how to be divine by being fully human.

St. Athanasius said that God became man so that man might become God. But this is in full communion with God, never independent of God, even when done in the name of God. There is no other way. Lucifer tried to become like God independently of God; therefore, he was alienated from God.

Jesus is the Christ, the Anointed One. He is anointed by the Spirit of God, the breath of God. We who follow him are Christians and anointed with the same Spirit. His breath becomes our life breath. His wind fills the sails of our life's ship; he propels us to heavenly shores.

Jesus is the Messiah, the One promised to lead his people into a new kingdom beyond all kingdoms. He brings final victory over his enemies in the midst of defeats and complete freedom to his spiritual Israel in the midst of slavery. He enables us to dwell in the Promised Land that includes and is beyond all lands.

Jesus is the Savior. We are like people who have fallen into a deep and desperate pit. He lifts us from the darkness and pulls us out into the daylight. If we have sunk beneath the waves of life's storms, he lifts us from the swell of the tempest. All we need to do is hold his hand. We are weak, but he is strong. We might lose our grip, but Jesus never loses his grip on us. He never lets us go.

Jesus is the Divine Rescue sent by the Father. God knows us better than we know ourselves because he is closer to us than we are to ourselves. In eternity beyond time and space, God knew that we would need help, that we would need to be rescued. He knew we would need to be saved. So he sent his Son. He sent Jesus to deliver us from a life and world of darkness and sin. He loves each of us so much that he died on a cross and rose from the dead for each one of us personally. He shed every drop of blood for you and me personally. The Rescue is intimate, personal, and powerful. He comes personally for each of us. When we receive that personally, it changes our lives forever.

Jesus is the Word. A word is the soul of a person passed on in spoken form. Words pass on being. Jesus is the very soul of the Father in the Spirit. He is the Word of words. He is every word in the one Word. He is the desire of every human being in pure Being. He is the Word in silence, and the divine Silence between the letters and sounds of every word. He changes how we listen and speak. He causes all sounds and letters to glimmer.

Jesus fulfills all. He complements and completes all truth without belittling any truth, and without giving into any half-truth. He does this so that all can know the fullness of Truth. He loves all and respects all. He completes all.

Jesus is the Way, the Truth, and the Life. All that came before him points to him. Only those who cannot give up their own partial truth resist him who is all Truth.

Jesus is the Word that defies all words but completes all words. He is the Idea that is beyond ideas but perfects all ideas. He is the Word in silence, the Communion in solitude, and the Mystery in plain sight.

Jesus is the Passion that lifts us above every impure passion and cleanses all passions. Good passion empowers our love of God. Bad passion distorts, distracts, and obstructs our vision of God because it directs us primarily toward ourselves as the focal point of creation. Good passion creates enthusiasm—that is, *en theos*, or "in God." Jesus is impassioned and wants his followers to be passionate.

How passionate are we today?

Jesus Is the Heart of God

Jesus is the heart of God and the heart of all humanity. He satisfies the longing of all hearts.

His sacred heart is pierced so that all hardened hearts might be pierced with love. His heart is broken yet heals every broken heart.

His heart is hidden and unseen in the Body of Christ but vital in bringing life to every active member of the Body.

His heart pumps the blood of God and humanity. His blood is shed to manifest the self-sacrificing love of God for all humanity. On the Cross Jesus lays down his life for everyone.

All who receive him into their hearts know him and share in his Body and Blood.

Have you received him?

Jesus: Mystery of Mysteries

Jesus is the Mystery of mysteries. This is visible in the communion of divinity and humanity in the Incarnation. The Spirit of the eternally begotten Son of the Father takes on flesh. He is incarnate, *in carne,* or "in meat." And Incarnation reaches its fullness on the Cross where life takes on death. There, eternal life is established through death, and glory is revealed in humiliation. Humanity's shame is fully clothed in his nakedness, which covers every naked soul. Every tear that is shed is shared and wiped away in his agony and cry.

Because Jesus is the Resurrection and the Life, death is clearly and objectively defeated once and for all. But it remains a mystery beyond human comprehension. It is pure miracle. His victory gives us courage and hope when we need them the most. It is the once-and-for-all victory cry of God for all humanity, the Uncreated for all creation!

The resurrected body of Jesus shows us where our bodies are destined in him. This, too, remains a mystery for us on this earth. He had physical form but could appear in a room without coming through the doorway. He could invite Thomas to put his finger into his wounds and could eat on the shore of the Sea of Galilee. Yet he could appear as himself or as a gardener.

Jesus is the new heavenly Jerusalem, with streets of gold but transparent as glass. He is fully in and beyond all dimensions of space and time, all at once. He is pure Humanity in space and time and in eternity.

Jesus is the ascended One. He prepares a place for those of earth in heaven. He prepares a place in eternity beyond space and time for those who are trapped in space and time. This is the time beyond time and the space beyond space that includes and surpasses all time and space. It is embodied beyond mere earthly bodies in a glorified body. Jesus assures us that the trials and struggles of this wink-of-an-eye in time and space are next to nothing when viewed from the promise of eternity.

Jesus sends the Holy Spirit from the Father to help us on our earthly journey. He breathes his life into the apostles to lead the Church, and then sends the Spirit like a mighty, rushing wind on the entire Church. He sends the power and dynamite. Without these, we cannot complete Christian life or any ministry, no matter how excited we are at first. He is the Tongue beyond all tongues yet proclaimed in all tongues. He is the Miracle in the mundane that makes all mundane things miraculous. He is the Extraordinary in the ordinary that transforms everything ordinary into the extraordinary. He makes all things new.

Jesus is the Bread of Life. He hides all the above and more in every Eucharist. Yet in every Eucharist he is revealed. His Body and Blood are fully present. He brings the Incarnation of two thousand years ago into the now at every Eucharist. He is the Priest in every priest, the Man in every man, woman, and child who faithfully receives him in Holy Eucharist.

The Love of Jesus

Jesus is divine love incarnate. His love is for each of us personally. He was born in a stable to enrich us through love—for me. He taught every teaching, worked every miracle, and even raised the dead out of love—for me. He died on a cross and shed every drop of blood out of love—for me. I often cross my hands over my heart as I sing or say the sacred words of the liturgy. I invite everyone into this personal encounter with Jesus Christ from the depths of your own heart.

In Jesus, the lights of humanity, which had been almost completely dimmed through sin, are turned on completely. They are brought up to the brightest possible illumination we can know on this earth at this time. How sad it is that we so often reduce him to far less than he is and settle for so very little when it comes to our experience and expression of Christian faith.

Jesus comes that we might have life abundantly and fully. He wants us to experience him as Catholics, from the word *catholicos*, meaning "universal and full."

Jesus is this and much, much more. What we understand as true is next to nothing when compared with the fullness of his being. The things we can understand and speak in part only point the way. We must still make the journey. He is the Companion on the way, and he is the final Destination.

What journey are you on?

Mary: Holy Is His Name

Let me set the scene. It was during an ordinary family breakfast in the home of dear friends. I was seated with seven or more kids at a large picnic table, which served as this large family's dining table. The mother was serving pancakes at a very fast pace. In my mind, it seemed as if they were being flown out to the table like Frisbees! Pancakes, butter, and syrup were flying everywhere. It was messy, just like family life often is. But it was also a scene of great love and joy as children giggled with glee at the wonders that only family and plenty of pancakes can bring!

I was glancing at my Roman Liturgy of the Hours prayer book, looking ahead to Evening Prayer. The Magnificat, or Canticle of Mary, caught my eye. There—in the midst of the pancakes, butter, syrup, and kids squealing with delight—my song "Holy Is His Name" was born. It came in a divine flash right there in the ordinary setting of an extraordinarily ordinary large breakfast.

Of the hundreds I have recorded, "Holy Is His Name" turned out to be one of my most popular songs. It is the song of Mary, the mother of Jesus. I have walked people through it thousands of times in concerts, retreats, and ministries around the world. Somehow Mary helps break down the barriers between believers from Catholic, Orthodox, and Protestant traditions.

Here is what I have often shared. It comes from the heart of Catholic Christianity, but it always seems to minister to everyone:

- Mary always points to Jesus.
- Mary is important because Jesus is *more* important.

- We venerate Mary and worship God.
- We venerate Mary as the saint of saints because we worship Jesus as God and man.

Mary is essential in the mystery of the Incarnation of God's Son, Jesus. Without Mary, Jesus would not have been born into this world. The Incarnation, the Divine Mediator, could not have happened without her full cooperation. Therefore redemption only occurred because of her cooperation.

Because of all of this, Mary is the greatest of all saints. We honor, or venerate, saints, but we worship God. Still, Mary is venerated in an extraordinary way because she gave birth to Jesus, God incarnate. She is not God, but without her God would not have come among us in the flesh.

Mary Our Mother

Just as scripture revealed that Jesus is the new Adam, the Church Fathers taught that Mary is the new Eve. The old Eve brought sin into the world through her disobedience; the new Eve brought righteousness into the world through her obedience. The first Eve tied the knot of disobedience for the old Adam, and the second Eve unties it for the new Adam to bring righteousness into the world.

Mary said yes to the work of the Holy Spirit announced through the angel Gabriel. She dared to believe what the world would say is impossible. She dared to believe that a child could be born without any human father at all. This is biologically impossible. She did not understand it, but she believed it. For Mary, all things are possible with God.

Mary is the *Theotokos*, the Godbearer. She is not the mother of God eternal or the eternally begotten Son of the Father in the Trinity. But she is the mother of Jesus on earth, and Jesus is fully God and fully man—the Son of God and the Son of Mary. She is the bearer of man and the mother of the Christ. But because God and man are one in Christ, she is also the Mother of God and the bearer of God.

We, too, must become bearers of God. It takes faith to believe the seemingly impossible. Scripture says that faith is the substance, the *hypostasis*, or personification of things hoped for, of things not yet seen. Mary is the mother of such faith.

Mary is a model of the Church. She is also the mother of the Church. John received her as his mother after the Crucifixion, and through his example we are called to receive her as well. Her yes is our yes, and her belief is our belief. As she received the word of the angel, so must we receive the

words of God's messengers in our lives. As the Holy Spirit
overshadowed her, so must we be overshadowed by God's
power. As she remained a virgin, so must we be set apart and
belong to God. As she saw the possible in the impossible,
so must we. And as she gave birth to Jesus, so must we give
birth to Jesus through our life in the Spirit.

Mary foreshadows the mystery of the Eucharist. As the
Spirit overshadowed her, so the elements of bread and wine
on the altar are overshadowed. As she conceived the Word-
made-flesh in her womb, so the ordained priest, through
speaking the Word, confects the Eucharist on the altar. As
she bore the Christ child in the stable and brought him into
the world, so the Eucharist, the very Body and Blood of Jesus
Christ, is made present to us. And as the shepherds and Magi
adored him, so must we.

Mary is inviolate. She is the Immaculate Conception. She
was conceived and kept from sin in her mother's womb so
that the child she bore would not inherit original ancestral
sin. Only then could he bear anyone's sin other than his own
on the Cross. He must be human to bear human sin, and he
must be God to bear all sin. God is his Father, and Mary is
his Mother. She was freed from the Law according to the
Law by him who fulfilled and surpassed the Law. He was
born under the Law in Mary to free those entrapped by it.

This is a bit of a mind-blowing time loop reaching back
to the saints of old and creating new ones for the future. It
was created by the One who is eternal and beyond time.
Mary was conceived and kept from sin so that Jesus could be
born without sin and bear the sins of the world on the Cross.

All of this was accomplished through the salvation of
Jesus Christ on the Cross. Mary was preserved from sin in
her mother's womb by the grace of the *future* atoning death
and resurrection of the Son she would bear. Mary is saved by
the Son she bore so that the Son could be born without sin in
order to bear the sins she would have otherwise committed

without his Cross. This miracle was done through grace. But we, too, are kept from sin by grace, though not in the same way as Mary. She physically bore Jesus into this world; we bear him in our hearts.

In Mary, all human life in the womb is shown to be precious. John the Baptist, while in Elizabeth's womb, leaped at the presence of Mary who carried Jesus in her womb. So we must leap at the presence of all human life in the womb. We must venerate all life from conception in the womb.

Mary is ever-virgin. She was impregnated by God through the Holy Spirit as a virgin and gave birth without violating that virginity. She was a virgin after the birth of Jesus as she was before. This is a mystery. It defies human logic and medical science. We are also called to be virginal. The Holy Spirit purifies us and restores our dignity. The Word is conceived in our lives, yet we remain virginal even after the birth of Christ in us or through us. We are children who will live in the company of Christ and be like him.

Mary was assumed into heaven, body and soul. Enoch and Elijah foreshadowed this because they "walked with God." St. Paul tells us that the wages of sin is death. Mary was without sin, so she was freed from the death of sin. Yet she also was privileged to share in her Son's death by "falling asleep." Many Christians call this the *dormition*. Mary then shared fully in the Resurrection and Ascension by being bodily assumed into heaven. Jesus is the Redeemer. Mary is redeemed but fully participates in his mission of redemption. She shares in redemption, both receiving it and bringing it to others. So must we share in the Resurrection as part of the redeemed, as sharers in his mission of redemption. We, too, will be rapt into heaven either at the end of our earthly lives or at the Second Coming of Christ.

Mary is the intercessor of the saints. As she interceded with Jesus at the wedding feast at Cana, she still intercedes for us now and at the hour of our death. When the wine of our lives runs out, Mary simply teaches us to do whatever Jesus tells us. If he tells us to haul water like the workers in Cana, we haul water. What he asks is often hard and exhausting work. But if we do it, Jesus changes the water of our ordinary lives into the wine of God's miracles. We, too, are called to intercede for one another and haul the water of daily virtues so that we all might become the miracles of God.

Mary is the pure glass through which the Son shines. She does not color the Son nor obstruct him. His light passes through her as through a window. We, too, must be a clear glass through which the Son of God may shine on the world.

Mary is the pure vessel in which the water of the Spirit and the Body and Blood of Christ come to you and me. There is nothing stained in her that would stain him. He comes to us purely through Mary because he has kept Mary pure through his Cross. We, too, are called to be pure because we bear Christ for the world.

When singing "Holy Is His Name," I ask the congregation to focus on the word *holy*, which means to be "set apart." I invite them to raise up their hands and let God raise them up above darkness, sin, and negativity. Mary reminds us to let God lift us up above our darkness and sin.

Where is your darkness, your sin, or your negativity today? Where do you feel the world and its cares pulling you down? Let Jesus lift you up from your darkness and set you apart for the wonderful and life-giving things of God right now. This is a big part of Mary's message for you.

Blessings and Beatitudes

The Church is the Body of Christ. Every body has a heart.

The heart of Jesus' teaching is the Sermon on the Mount, and the heart of the Sermon is the Beatitudes. *Beatitude* simply means "blessing." A blessing is like an island that stands untouched whether the waters are smooth or stormy. The Beatitudes are blessings that cannot be stopped or corrupted by the curse of sin. Even more, they can deliver us from the curse of sin.

"Blessed are the poor in spirit" (Mt 5:3). We find wealth in poverty, and poverty in too much wealth. We find the kingdom of heaven.

"Blessed are they who mourn" (Mt 5:4). We find comfort in our sorrow, and sorrow in superficial happiness. We are comforted.

"Blessed are the meek" (Mt 5:5). We find glory in humility, and we are humbled in our glory. We inherit the Promised Land of God.

"Blessed are they who hunger and thirst for righteousness" (Mt 5:6). We are filled with righteousness when we hunger for it. The more we obtain it, the more we hunger and thirst for it.

"Blessed are the merciful" (Mt 5:7). We find mercy when we show it. The more we show mercy to others, the more we realize that we ourselves need mercy. We are merciful because we have been shown mercy by God. His mercy comes from his innermost being.

"Blessed are the pure in heart" (Mt 5:8, *NRSV*). The heart is our innermost being, our deepest selves, the center of our selves. It is there that we see God. God is a fire that purifies, and warms. The more we see God, the more we are purified in his fiery presence.

"Blessed are the peacemakers" (Mt 5:9). We bring peace in the midst of conflict, violence, and war. But often the more we bring peace to others, the more others (and the demons) oppose and even make war on us. We are children of God after the example of God's Son, who was rejected before he was received.

"Blessed are they who are persecuted for the sake of righteousness" (Mt 5:10). We may be persecuted when we follow Jesus Christ, but we have peace within. The more we have peace within, the more we spread it to others, the more we are persecuted. This is the way of the prophets. It was also the way of Jesus.

Together, these form the heart of the Jesus' teaching. They are blessings. They are the Beatitudes.

God Alone

Let's continue with the basics, but also reach a bit higher.

I often sing the song "God Alone Is Enough" at the beginning of an evening of prayer. After doing some uplifting songs of praise, I like to lead the congregation into something more meditative.

Worship and praise are upward motions of releasing our whole being to God. They involve opening ourselves up to God who inhabits, or is enthroned upon, our praises. Meditation is a downward movement of the Spirit that releases us completely for God. In both we let go of our old selves in order to become new creations. This is the core of our Christian experience.

Worship and praise involve letting go of ourselves through motions that are energetic, upward, and outward toward God. Meditation and contemplation involve letting go of the old self by letting it drop away like an old set of clothes that no longer fits our soul very well. Only then does a new person emerge who is the person God originally created us to be when we were first conceived in our mother's womb.

The Word *Monk*

What does it mean to say, "God alone is enough?"

I first encountered monks in a Carmelite monastery in Munster, Indiana. It is a beautiful place, with grottos and walkways that wind through the Stations of the Cross. I did not dare talk to the monks, or Carmelite friars. I was simply aware that they walked in a silence that drew me closer to Jesus. Later I would meet Franciscan friars who incarnated that ideal in a very welcoming and warmly human way.

Along my faith journey, I met monks and sisters of many kinds, including Benedictines, Cistercians, Camaldolese, Carthusians, and Eastern. I found that a common thread of radical Gospel living ran through all their unique charisms and expressions. This charism is what fires my heart in Christ and the Church. It is the calling to which I am called, and that I share with those of all states of life today.

This leads us to the word *monk*. *Monk* comes from the Greek *monos*, meaning "alone." Anytime you see *alone* in scripture, the Greek word is *monos*.

Monos is used to describe hermits who are literally alone. It is also used for those who live "alone" together, in communities of monks. It can be used to describe those of us who are seeking God alone as the source and summit of our entire lives. There is a little monk inside every serious Catholic Christian, in every state of life. Some live it out literally in monastic communities. Some affiliate with monastic communities while staying in the secular world. Some do so privately. All can be radical.

The monk renounces all to gain everything.

The monk is "separated from all, and united with all."

The monk is poor in order to know the wealth of God, creation, and humanity.

The monk is obedient to discover real freedom.

The monk is chaste to know real communion and community.

The monk is stable in an unstable and transient world, and can touch all people with grace.

The monk does penance through ongoing conversion of life, so that others might come to know God.

All this flows from the paradox of the Cross and Resurrection of Jesus, and the fullness of God's love.

God is not a masochist. He does not delight in making us give up interacting with people or having things for the sake of renunciation. He is not a demented puppeteer. Renunciation is only a tool that leads us to greater abundance. We renounce all to gain everything.

Jesus comes that we might have life and have it abundantly. We gain thirty-, sixty-, and a hundredfold for every thing, person, or situation of which we let go for God.

We let go of three things: things, people, and ourselves.

We let go of things not because the created world is bad but because we so often use it badly. Then we are possessed by our possessions and consumed by the things we consume. When we renounce possessions, we can become real stewards of creation. We can fully enjoy creation only after we have renounced it.

We let go of relationships not because relationships are bad but because we so often engage in relationships badly. Jesus blesses marriage at the wedding feast in Cana. It is his first public miracle. But he also asks all his followers to renounce mother, father, wife, and children for his sake. Our past patterns of relationship often enable bad behavior rather than empower Christlike behavior. When we renounce past patterns of failed relationship, our relationships can prosper in Christ.

Lastly, and most importantly, we must renounce ourselves. This is not because the human being is bad. God created us in his image and likeness! It is because we have lost that likeness and settled for a version of ourselves that is not the person God created us to be. We renounce the old self so that we can be created anew, born again, and raised up as a new creation in Christ. Only when we renounce ourselves for Christ can we discover who we really are.

That is what the essence of being a monk really is.

The Fathers say that everyone who serves Jesus without compromise is a monk in spirit. Is there a monk in you today?

The Painter

In the early days of my Christian music ministry, I released a project called *The Painter*. It was originally intended to be part of another project that we eventually called *The Lord's Supper*. I was going to call the album *The Painter, Mass in the Key of D Major*, but the record company was hesitant about two things: releasing a double recording at that point in my career, and calling it a Mass because my audience was ecumenical. So we first released the Mass under the title *The Lord's Supper*. When it quickly became a big hit, I teamed up with my brother, Terry, to finish *The Painter*. It was also a best seller; it is considered by some to be a landmark recording in the Christian music of that era. Both projects form a dual expression of a similar style, one with a choir and the other with my brother. I remain proud of them both.

The analogy of Jesus as a painter had long interested me. I loved it when writers used similar themes, and there had been a few best sellers among them in both the secular and religious worlds. I decided to try it with music.

Jesus is like a master painter. He paints our lives better than anyone else.

We are like a canvas for the Painter. The canvas must be chosen and prepared before the painting begins, or the work will be in vain. It is stretched on a frame. It is cleaned. We are also stretched by Jesus and cleansed of sin before he paints our lives.

The Holy Spirit is his brush. Religion alone cannot paint anything of beauty, but religion must be included to give form to the Spirit.

The fruits of the Spirit are the various colors he uses. He colors our lives with

- love as self-emptying where there is self-absorption and hatred;
- joy that comes from a whole new way of life instead of the sadness of self-centeredness and frustration;
- peace that surpasses all understanding where there is inner conflict from resisting letting go of the old self;
- patience where there is the impatience of wanting one's own way in everything;
- kindness where there is the callousness of an intractable self;
- mildness where there is the coarseness of only thinking of oneself;
- generosity where there is the hoarding of possessions and emotional wealth through selfishness;
- chastity and self-control where there is impurity and self-indulgence at the cost of others; and
- faith where there is doubt rooted in believing only what is natural and carnal.

These fruits of the Spirit only appear on the canvas of our life when we let the old self die through the Cross of Jesus and rise up as wholly new in the Spirit through the Resurrection of Jesus. The Cross is the key. The Resurrection is the inner room we enter where we fully encounter Jesus in deep prayer.

He also colors us with love as it is described by St. Paul in 1 Corinthians 13: Love is patient. Love is kind. Love is humble and does not put on airs in arrogance. Love is never rude. Love does not insist on its own way. Love is not irritable or resentful. It does not rejoice at wrong but rejoices in the truth. Love bears all things, believes all things, hopes all things, endures all things. Love never ends. In the end, only faith, hope, and love abide. Of these three, the greatest is love.

Jesus paints us with the living paradoxes described in the Beatitudes and the Sermon on the Mount. These are the things for which the human heart hungers. And we are restless and frustrated until we find them.

It is not enough to just get our doctrine or religion right. We must allow religion—with all its practices, disciplines, laws, traditions, and prayers—to lead us to the real beauty of the Holy Spirit and to reflect the beauty of life in the Holy Spirit.

Sometimes we let something or someone other than God paint our lives. The world can paint our lives. Our egos can paint our lives. Our carnality can paint our lives. But while these always promise beauty, they end up flawed, ugly, and dark. If we open ourselves to Jesus, he will paint over the ugly and flawed things of our lives with the beautiful colors of the Holy Spirit and the Gospel.

Jesus is the master painter. Are we allowing him to color our lives with the colors of the Holy Spirit? Are we allowing Jesus to make us into something beautiful for God?

Surrender to Jesus

It is through surrender to Jesus that we find his victory in life. Sin is defeated, and we are set free!

I wrote "Surrender to Jesus" while walking an itinerant ministry from our Little Portion Monastery to Little Rock. We walked 150 miles in poverty and total availability, stopping at churches along the way. We had been taken in at a local Catholic church in Clinton, Arkansas, about halfway to our destination.

While we walked the fifteen or so miles a day, together we recited traditional Catholic prayers and litanies, and sang contemporary charismatic worship songs. It lifted our spirits during the very long walks with aching muscles and lots of sweat in the hot Arkansas sun.

One of the old prayer books we had with us contained two prayers written by St. Ignatius of Loyola: Surrender, or *Suscipe*, and the Anima Christi. While sitting outside in the shade of a tree near the back door of the church in Clinton, I put both of these wonderful prayers to music. I have used "Surrender to Jesus" in concerts ever since.

I often share what I found compelling in the song before I sing it.

In the earthly world, to surrender means that we are defeated; we will be taken prisoner, perhaps tortured or forced to say things that we do not believe. But in the kingdom of God, to surrender means that we share in the victory of Jesus, maybe for the first time in our lives, for the first time in a long time, or maybe just for the first time today. In Jesus, surrender means victory!

Surrender means letting go of your old self through the Cross of Jesus. We stop fighting. We give up. We let go and let God. Only then can we be resurrected and rise up a new person in Christ.

We had to surrender on those penitential prayer walks. We surrendered our desire for cool shade or a simple glass of water, and to tired backs and aching muscles. But once we surrendered these things to Jesus and focused on Jesus— Jesus alone—they seemed to demand much less of our attention. Then a cool glass of water while sitting in the shade seemed like heaven on earth! We never took those things for granted again, or at least not until the memory of the walk and the surrender to Jesus began to fade. Then we stirred up the memory, and we were set free from our daily aches, pains, struggles, and trials by surrendering to Jesus once again.

Surrender to Jesus and share in his victory. It is the victory of love over self-obsession and sin, peace over inner and outer conflict, forgiveness over judgment, justice over vengeance, and meekness over ego and pride. This is a victory we all long for. Find it by surrendering to Jesus right now.

Sand Dunes and the Holy Spirit

The first sand dunes I ever saw were on the southeastern shores of Lake Michigan. Since then, I have seen them on the shores of oceans and in the desert. I have often sat and watched the wind sweep across the dunes, mesmerized by their shifting patterns and shapes. Yet both the wind and the dunes have remained as something constant and solid.

The wind blows in from the water over the sand dunes. It is irresistible and strong. It blows across the sands on the shore, making beautiful patterns. It builds up the dunes, some huge, reaching like mountains to the sky. But the wind is always changing, always creating new sand paintings from God and building up new sand dunes like cathedrals on the shore. Only the wind and the sand remain constant.

The relationship between the Holy Spirit and religion is like the wind and sand dunes. The Spirit is always blowing from the infinite water of eternity across the shores of space and time. The Spirit creates beautiful sand patterns, created by the hand of God. The Spirit raises up tall and mighty sand dunes like cathedrals on the shores of time. These forms are the religious expressions of humanity, for humanity, created by the Spirit of God.

Religion often pours concrete over these beautiful patterns and sand dunes to remind us of God's wonders and to preserve them for the future. In itself, this is not a bad thing.

But this reminder of God's past wonders can blind us to the wonders of God's Spirit in the present. While we obsess about the concrete and the patterns of the past, we often miss the real fluidity of the work of the Holy Spirit happening among us today. At times, we criticize the new work because it does not conform exactly to the patterns of the past. When the wind of the Spirit has not been able to shape concrete, it has moved elsewhere, down the shore to create new sand patterns and mighty dunes.

Are we appreciative of the patterns of the past but also open to the ones of the present, as we build creatively to a new future in Christ and the Church? This only happens when there is a balance between ancient structures of old and the free work of the Spirit in the here and now.

The Holy Spirit and Freeze-Dried Coffee

My spiritual father liked a good cup of coffee. Many of our best times came early in the morning as the sun rose over the Alverna Franciscan Center. He would drink his coffee, and I would drink my tea. Good conversation about God ensued.

He didn't really like freeze-dried coffee. He said that it tasted artificial. But being a good teacher, he found in it a useful example for life in the Spirit and in the Church.

He would say that the fire of the Holy Spirit is like hot water, and freeze-dried coffee is like religion without the Holy Spirit. You have to pour hot water into the freeze-dried coffee to unlock its power to make coffee you can actually drink.

The same is true with religion. Religion without the fire of the Holy Spirit is like freeze-dried coffee. You cannot drink it. If you try to eat it, it tastes terrible. But if you add hot water, it becomes a cup of coffee that you can drink. The flavor of the coffee is unlocked.

But hot water without the freeze-dried coffee is also incomplete. You must have the substance of the freeze-dried coffee granules to complete the hot water, to make a cup of coffee.

Religion without the Holy Spirit is lifeless and tastes terrible. But the Holy Spirit without religion has no form. It is not fully incarnational. Jesus is the Incarnation, and to follow him we must be the same.

Water Drops and the Sun

The work of the Holy Spirit is like water drops and sunbeams. When it rains, the raindrops cause sunbeams to glisten in midair. They can even create the beauty of a rainbow. There are wonderful spiritual lessons in this for us and for the Church.

The first is that God the Father is like the sun. The emanating sunbeams are like Jesus, the Son of God, who came from God. Raindrops are like the power of the Spirit. But it is the raindrops that cause the sunbeams to become visible in a brilliant and beautiful way. The sun shines through the water and begins to sparkle and shimmer, even taking on the colors of the rainbow. The power of the Holy Spirit in our lives is similar. It is the Holy Spirit that causes the presence of Jesus to sparkle in our lives. The Spirit brings God's beautiful colors into a person's soul. Without the raindrops, the sunbeam is real and brings much life, but it does not glisten with power and light.

The second lesson turns this analogy around. The human soul is like a drop of water. By itself it is wonderful, but it is often colorless. It is only when the sun shines through it that it begins to glisten and manifest beautiful colors. Here, the sunbeams represent the work of the Holy Spirit, which is sometimes unseen, taken for granted until it illuminates an object or leaves a shadow. It takes the drop of water—the human soul—to bring out the sunbeams' brilliance and color.

Of course, this imagery can be extended again to the Church. The Church has a definite structure but a fluid form, like a drop of water. But it takes the sunbeam to cause it to glisten and take on beautiful living color.

Are we allowing the Holy Spirit to bring the spiritual color of the Spirit into our lives? Do we permit the real power of the Spirit to cause our whole lives to glisten with God? Is our parish or community glistening and coming into living color with the Holy Spirit, or do we just plod through the liturgy and our ministry in a flat and lifeless way?

Two Wings of the Dove

The balance between the Spirit and religion is like the two wings of a dove.

A dove needs two wings to fly. If it only has one wing, it cannot soar to the heavens. It will only flap its wing in vain and wear itself out.

Religion without the power of the Holy Spirit cannot fly. It cannot soar to the heavens. It can only flap around on the ground. Eventually it wears itself out and dies. Religion alone denies the power of the Holy Spirit and enslaves rather than empowers people on earth. Likewise, the Holy Spirit without religion has no form. It cannot affect anything on earth with the Gospel of Jesus Christ. Those who say they are "spiritual but not religious" are living an illusion and are eventually disillusioned.

As soon as a gathering of believers does anything in common, they are a religion. As soon as they follow even an informal "order of service," they are liturgical. This is not bad. It is simply part of being human and living in the created world.

What we need is religion and the Holy Spirit. We need two wings to fly, to soar to the heavens as the dove of God. Do we sometimes try to fly to the heavens with only one wing on the body of our spiritual life?

Love and Truth

Again, love and truth, or the Spirit and the Law, are like two wings a dove needs to fly upward.

Many of us are adamant about truth when it applies to someone else. But when truth is applied to our own conduct or life, we often try to dodge the bullet or beg mercy and forgiveness. We are often very judgmental of others but demand mercy and forgiveness for ourselves. This is not the authentic Gospel of Jesus Christ.

I believe that Western culture is in a period of darkness regarding truth. Some truth is universal, some is relative in applying the universal, and some is still to be developed. But we are in a crisis of truth today. Many prophecies regard a period where the world is handed over to Satan before the return of Christ. Today certainly feels like at least a partial fulfillment of those prophecies. What used to be wrong is now right, and what used to be right is now wrong. This confusion comes from the devil. He is the father of lies and confusion. This confusion breaks down families, culture, religious and monastic communities, and even the Church in a particular culture. It breaks down our ability to believe that a commitment by anyone really is trustworthy.

But in the end we have a choice: we can curse the darkness or light a candle. I choose to do the latter. I choose to love, trust, and forgive rather than watch out for myself, doubt, and judge. That is the way of Christ, the apostles, and the saints.

Is this your way as well?

PART TWO

The Inner Room

Known and Unknown

We travel in the Spirit to God in stages, both knowable and unknowable. Sometimes this is called the active and contemplative life.

The active life involves lectio divina: *lectio* (sacred reading), *oratio* (prayer), and *meditatio* (meditation). It involves asceticism and all the disciplines we know how to practice.

Contemplation, or *contemplatio*, is the fourth stage added to the other three. The contemplative life builds on the active life; it includes and goes beyond it. It goes into unknowing and divine darkness. We progress through the stages, but never leave the preceding stages behind. We experience all of them.

At first God speaks to us through things we can grasp with senses, images, and thoughts. In his great love, he reaches out to us in immanence, in what is closest to us. These things are knowable, and we can know God in part through them. These things are part of what we call cataphatic theology: the positive things we know and can say about God.

But as we progress, we come to the things of God that are beyond all knowledge, the divine unknowing. God in his fullness is beyond our comprehension and our ability to describe or speak about. We can say more about what God is not than what he is. This is what we call negative, or apophatic theology.

The first way has to do with God's uncreated energies. The second has to do with his essence. His essence exists in all his uncreated energies. No one can fully know God's essence in this life and stay on earth. We would have to pass over to the other side to gaze on such things, and even there we can never fully know the essence of God.

When we look directly into the sun, we are blinded. Likewise, when we look directly into the uncreated light of God, we often think we see nothing at all. We see only darkness, but it is the divine darkness.

God is a form beyond all forms and an image beyond all images. He is pure mystery that explains all that is and all that can be.

We set out on these stages of spiritual growth under the direction of a spiritual father or mother, an elder, or a spiritual director. They guide us and help us avoid missteps. They pass on what they have received from their fathers and mothers, as we become their spiritual children. But the point is our growth in God, not stages or elders.

Let us set out on this journey. Let us journey to God.

True Love

The most important charism of my community, the Brothers and Sisters of Charity, is love. This is also true of the Church, and any community or family in God. Jesus teaches us that the love of God and neighbor is the fulfillment of the whole Law and all the prophets. The apostle Paul tells us that it is the greatest charismatic gift; he places it first on his list of the fruit of the Holy Spirit. Therefore love is the greatest charism and our most important law in the community. When you cannot find a law or a leader to guide you in what to do, follow the advice of St. Augustine who said, "Love God and do what you will." We must ask, "What would Jesus do?"

Love is most fully manifested in the self-gift of Jesus Christ on the Cross. Love is not the annihilation of self but rather the *sacrifice* of self. You cannot sacrifice what you do not first possess. Therefore, a true and humble love of self must precede self-sacrifice. As Jesus teaches, "Love your neighbor as yourself" (Mt 22:39).

True love of self is based on the love of God who created us in his image. That image has been obscured by sin, but God's image remains in us and is restored once we are cleansed from sin in Christ. We must hate sin if we love God, but hatred of self does injustice to the image of God. Injustice to the image of God is a sin against God himself. In order to love God, we must love ourselves. If we love ourselves, we will appreciate ourselves, honor the image of God within us, and develop a positive self-image.

Yet genuine self-sacrifice brings an even greater self-fulfillment. As Jesus says, "Whoever finds his life will lose it, and whoever loses his life for my sake will find it" (Mt 10:39). Therefore a true self-sacrifice brings both true self-fulfillment and the paradox of the Cross, the ultimate fulfillment of self through selfless love.

Authentic self-awareness in the mystery of Christ does not make us egotistical or proud. It makes us humble. Humility is absolutely necessary in community. This humility must be based on truth of our own self-existence in light of the truth of God. All humankind bears the image of God; the Church as the temple of the Holy Spirit is the Body of Christ, and all creation also bears God's traces. It is true that we are dependent on God, and interdependent within the Church, the human race, and the created world for our very existence. This truth of our own existence fosters both humility and a sense of positive self-worth.

The humility of love fosters neither independence nor codependency in community. Independence denies our dependence on God and our interdependency within the Church, the human race, and the created world. It is ultimately egotistical and proud. Codependency seeks a false helplessness, a dependency on God and people as a reaction to a lack of true appreciation of self or positive self-image. Ultimately it causes unrealistic expectations in our relationship with God and with people, and leads to disappointment, despair, and even hatred. Attitudes of independence and codependency work in opposition to the true charism of love, which fosters the attitude of humility based on truth. Since true humility is necessary in community, a mature attitude of self-love and self-worth in the Lord, which breeds a positive self-image, is needed by all.

If we are truly humble, we will realize our interdependence with others and our dependence on God. It also leads us to silence so we can better listen to God and to other people. The choice to be silent is based on love, which calls us to sacrifice the self through silence so that the words of others might be truly heard.

If we really listen in silence to others and to God, then we will discover the gift of obedience. Obedience involves simply and maturely cooperating with the reality of our dependence on God and our interdependency with people, especially those in the offices of authority established by God within the Church and the world. This holds true especially in the Church and the communities of the Church who guide us in the name of God toward our self-fulfillment in Christ. It also flows from the self-sacrifice of love, in which the self willingly conforms to the self-sacrifice of Jesus Christ on the Cross.

The Lover and the Beloved

When I first became a Catholic Christian I was shocked and then pleasantly surprised and inspired to find that our life in Christ compared to a spousal relationship between a husband and wife. We find this spousal mysticism first in scripture regarding the Church, then regarding patristics in the writings of St. Augustine, and then with St. Bernard of Clairvaux and St. Bonaventure regarding the individual soul. Some of it is quite explicit. This understanding reaches its fullest expression in St. John of the Cross. And now many of those from Protestant traditions are finding inspiration from the analogy.

Spiritual life is like a lover and his beloved. It is a spousal mysticism. We are the bride of Christ. This is true both on the communal level as a Church and on the personal level in private devotion and prayer.

The first stage of any love relationship is attraction and dialogue. The attraction is electric. It is mysterious and almost irresistible. It defies logic or scientific description. This is like the mystical spark of the Holy Spirit that attracts us to Jesus Christ, the Church, and deeper prayer. It is a mystery as to how, when, or even why it works. We can explain it in part, but never fully.

But a romantic couple must move from initial attraction to dialogue very quickly. They must talk about objective facts. Where are they from? What do they do for a living? What are their likes and dislikes? Where do they want to live?

This is like the dialogue we have with the Church, the communities or ministries of the Church, a good spiritual director, and trusted spiritually orthodox friends. In such exchanges we discern the fruits of objective doctrine regarding faith and morality. We learn the good external disciplines that promote and purify our inner lives, and gain the necessary tools to discern whether or not the Spirit to whom we are listening is really Jesus. There are many false spirits who have imitated Jesus, but they are angels of darkness masked as angels of light. Doctrine and discipline are the first objective tools in this discernment. They help us dialogue with Jesus.

After a time of discernment, the couple marries and consummates their union. This is a love union; it is beyond dialogue. It is emotional and passionate, but it is not selfish. It is the complete emptying of self for the sake of another. It is complete self-giving. Yet in self-emptying for the other, each is fulfilled.

This is like the charismatic and ecstatic mystical union of the Lover and the beloved. We are impregnated by the Spirit and grow with the fruit of the Spirit. We are lifted up out of ourselves for the sake of the Other. This is emotional, passionate—and holy. We enter this union with the complete emptying of self for the sake of Jesus. Yet in this self-emptying we are completely fulfilled. We are rapt of the self for the sake of God.

After the love union comes afterglow. It is a time of simple rest with each other, often described as the sweetest and most intimate time between husband and wife. No words are spoken. Such a love union is not repeated too soon; they are simply learning how to be with one another in complete rest.

This is like the contemplative stage in spiritual life. It follows the ecstatic union, mystical rapture, and charismatic high. Yet it is the most intimate time between the soul and Jesus. No words are spoken; they would intrude. The charismatic and mystical high of this love union is not repeated. We simply learn how to *be* with the One Who *Is*. This stage is beyond words, ideas, or forms, and no one can know it except the one who has experienced it. Words fall short.

After the consummation of the union and afterglow, a mature couple who is familiar with this process gets up to take care of the household. Using traditional descriptions, the wife gets the kids up and ready for school. The husband—and also nowadays, the wife—goes off to work to support the family.

This is the work of ministry and evangelization in the Church and the world. We give birth to many children of God through our union with Christ. We have married Jesus, consummated the marriage, been impregnated by the Spirit, and given birth to many children. Now we must take care of them. We wake and ready the house. We feed the children. We teach the younger ones. We support the older ones in their work.

Jesus has gone off to work. Sometimes it seems as if he is gone more than he is home. But he is supporting the household. We know that he will come back at the end of the day, and the process will repeat itself.

Finding Your Monastic Cell, Skete, or Monastery

The cell is the natural habitat for the monk. It is the protected haven of solitude and silence. Everyone must find their own inner cell, and a sacred worship space as well.

The root words for *cell* mean "a small hidden room, storeroom, or hut that conceals in order to save." In English, some have said that the word *cell* comes from the same root as the word *celestial* does. The word *cell* applies to individual monastic dwellings and small monasteries. It can also apply to any serious Christian's special prayer room or corner.

The monk's cell is celestial. In monastic thinking, it is the place where heaven comes down to earth. It is the monk's haven and heaven. It is ordinary but imbued with an extraordinary gift.

Just as fish die without water, so the monk dies outside of his cell. To understand the cell, all we need do is go into our cell, which will teach us everything. Sitting in the cell, we find stability. We do not leave it or our meditation with every little whim that crosses our minds. Stability in the cell teaches us all we need to know of monastic life.

I sit in my cell and allow my old self to be destroyed completely. Only then can I be born again as the child God originally intended me to be. The cell reflects the soul. An uncluttered cell symbolizes and assists an uncluttered soul. A cluttered cell causes the cluttered and distracted soul to grow even worse.

I am often tempted to leave my cell to converse with others or engage in some seemingly holy activity. But as often as I do so, I return less of a man.

Those who are often in the cell desire it all the more.
Those who are seldom in the cell tire of it quickly. Those who
are afraid of the solitude of the cell should beware of relationships with others. Those who are afraid of the responsi-
bility of loving relationships with others should beware of
the solitude of the cell. You cannot run from God in the cell.
And you cannot run from God in activity. Monastic life is a
full-on encounter with God.

Those who use a cell to run from the world or themselves are deluded. You cannot outrun yourself. The cell is
the place of naked and honest encounter with Reality. Those
who try to run from Reality in the cell will find it intolerable.
If we are worthy of the cell, it will welcome us. If we are
unworthy of the cell, it will spew us out.

The cell is the place for a naked encounter of the soul
with God. You cannot hide there. There are no ministries or
projects, activities or distractions, behind which to hide. The
cell is a place to encounter God alone.

It is also the place of spiritual battle with the soul's own
evils and ego attachments. These evils and ego attachments
often hide behind the activity and noise of both secular life
and ministry. In the cell, they rise to the surface like dross
rising from heated metal and must be addressed.

The cell is the forging furnace of the monk's soul. It is a
crucible where we are forged and shaped. Its heat can seem
unbearable. But the heat is necessary to soften the metal of
our heart and forge us into an instrument for God. Stability
in the cell makes us hard as iron. Instability of mind or activity in the cell makes a soul as soft as lead.

As a young monk, you need an experienced guide to
help you navigate the dangers of the soul's battle with its
evils in the cell. Without a spiritual father or mother to help
you, the cell can be a place of delusion.

Young monastics gather around a spiritual father,
mother, or elder. Likewise, individual cells are grouped

around the cell of the father, mother, or elder. Many monks live in monasteries as they lived in the world—in need of a spiritual father or mother to keep them honest in their calling. This is tragic.

It is better to live a holy life in the secular world than to live like a secular in a monastery. It is better to be an honestly seeking non-Christian than to be a bad Christian. It is better not to promise silence and solitude than to promise it and not keep it. To long for the secular world while in the cell is to desecrate the cell. It will not allow you to remain there. It will spew you out.

In order for monastics to stay close to their spiritual father or mother, the cells are grouped around a common chapel and common buildings. This is called a *laura, skete,* or *kellion.* The formation is patterned on the Middle Eastern *souk,* or market. It is a place where we trade with one another in the goods and riches of heaven. The skete integrates solitude with community, silence with speech, and the sacred stillness of the contemplative life with the activity of ministry.

The monastery is built around a rule and a spiritual father or mother. It is more communal by nature, with daily prayer, work, meals, and frequent teaching from the spiritual father or mother.

The average soul that goes prematurely into the solitude of the hermit's cell is destined for failure. Only the rarest of saints have ventured there at the beginning. Most seekers begin in the monastery. From there they go to the skete. From the skete they may venture into the solitude of the hermitage, first for a few days, then for the week, with returns to the monastery on Saturday and Sunday, and finally into the strict reclusion of the hermit's cell.

The monastery and skete are safe harbors of the soul. There we have not reached the dock of heaven yet. But we have come in from the rough waters of the secular world around the protective harbor wall.

The Spiritual Father and Mother

A monastery is a spiritual family. God is our Father, and the Church, as modeled by Mary, is our Mother. We also have spiritual fathers and mothers in Christ and the Church.

The spiritual father or mother helps give birth to us in Christ in monastic life. We may have many spiritual directors and elder brothers and sisters. We only have one spiritual father or mother.

The spiritual father or mother may be lay or cleric, and even monastic or secular, though the monastic tradition best illustrates this spiritual dynamic. Spiritual mothers or fathers are not sacramental confessors, nor are they psychological counselors, but they help us with sin and psychological health. They help us with our spiritual life.

They walk with us and ahead of us on our spiritual path in Christ. They point out the safest places to walk and the dangerous pitfalls to avoid. They do not lord it over the spiritual son or daughter. They assist us.

The guidance of the spiritual father or mother is both formal and informal. Their formal role is described in the rules and constitution of the monastery. Their informal role is more personal, gifting influence over the monastic's internal life in unperceivable ways. Spiritual fathers and mothers must fulfill their formal obligations as teachers and guides, but do not deny their experience, and help in informal ways when voluntarily invited by the aspiring or even older monastic.

To best provide spiritual guidance, a spiritual father or mother must know our deepest thoughts as well as the details of our external life. This requires revelation—we must share our thoughts and actions with them. We *confess* sins to a sacramental confessor. We *reveal* sins *and* temptations to our spiritual father or mother.

For the relationship not to become coercive, this revelation of thoughts in the internal forum is done voluntarily, and as each spiritual child is ready for such revelation. This requires spiritual trust. Those who break such trust can damage the spiritual child, sometimes even for life.

The ancient Fathers teach us that it is better to have a spiritual father or mother than not to have one. But it is also better to have no spiritual father or mother than to have a bad one. In that case, the teaching of the ancients guides us. But we should seek a good father or mother to be fully born again.

Spiritual fathers and mothers can lead only as they have first followed their own spiritual fathers or mothers. They speak from experience, not theory, and even less from ego.

Spiritual fathers and mothers exist under the higher authority of God and are mediated by the Church. They are not authoritative arbiters or lone rangers. They also live in community, which has checks and balances to keep them from falling into error and leading others astray. So we can safely follow true spiritual fathers and mothers.

Spiritual fathers and mothers do not assign themselves the role. That would be pride. When they are ready for such ministry, the calling is made clear. If a person put themselves forward as a spiritual father or mother prematurely, great folly and vanity follow. It does not bear spiritual fruit. It comes to nothing. Yet once called by God, the person must be bold enough to step out in answer to this call by making themselves available.

Conversely, as the old Eastern axiom says, when the disciple is ready, the master appears. The Spirit draws us to a community or spiritual father or mother. It is a work of grace, love, and spiritual attraction. It requires a supernatural readiness on the part of father, mother, and child. This includes and surpasses the mere logic of a counselor or confessor. It is something spiritual, supernatural, and mystical.

The terms *spiritual father* and *spiritual mother* are used literally and symbolically. They are realities and analogies. We use the language of *father*, *mother*, and *family* to describe spiritual and monastic life because the family is the most basic unit to civilization.

Today this assumption is not so assured. As the modern nuclear family breaks down in the West, the use of *father* and *mother* becomes more problematic. At times, would-be disciples project hurts from earthly fathers, mothers, and families onto a spiritual father, mother, or community. That can make the relationship difficult, even impossible.

Sometimes, though, the spiritual father, mother, and family can heal those hurts. The monastery can become a place of healing and wholeness. But this can be very difficult, sometimes seeming impossible and requiring nothing short of a miracle. Much patience and perseverance are required for such healing to occur.

Do you seek a spiritual father, mother, elder, or spiritual director to properly learn from? Do you realize that, truly, all things are possible with God? Miracles do happen!

Charismatic Praise and Thanksgiving

We have talked about praise and thanksgiving. We have seen the connection between positive or negative thoughts, emotions, words, and actions. We have seen the positive effect of praise and thanksgiving in the spiritual life.

In contemplative prayer we release the old self through a downward outpouring motion of releasing and letting go. Praise and thanks, however, have the ability to throw off the false self in a powerful upward motion. It is like a wave offering to God (see Exodus 29:24).

But what happens when our thoughts and emotions have become so habitually negative that it seems humanly impossible to break free? This is where the power of charismatic praise and thanksgiving comes in. Sometimes this form of prayer just involves praise with extra passion and spirit. Sometimes it means praying in tongues or praying in the Spirit.

Scripture and tradition describe two ways of speaking in tongues. One is the experience of Pentecost, where "tongues of fire" fell upon the assembled church, and they spoke in tongues so that people of every language could understand them. This form of speech is sometimes called *xenolalia*. It is for the good of those who hear.

In his first letter to the Corinthians, St. Paul describes another form of speaking in tongues. There he speaks of praying and singing in a way beyond human comprehension that is primarily for the good of those who do it. This form of speech is called *glossolalia*. While some of the Church Fathers indicated that this gift seemed absent from the more established Church of their postapostolic era, they continued to describe clearly charismatic experiences in the cathedrals of their time. In their writings, both St. Augustine in the West and St. John Chrysostom in the East describe singing in the Spirit as *jubilation*, when the congregation spontaneously sings praises to God without any common melody or words. They simply sing alleluias or vowel sounds. They describe the singing as so loud that it could be heard to the outskirts of their cities and towns. These descriptions certainly sound like contemporary singing in the Spirit to me!

This second form is what we often experience at a charismatic prayer meeting or church today. On a common psychological level, this kind of prayer is helpful for when we cannot seem to turn our mind to the positive, no matter how well we understand the principle or how hard we try. We temporarily bypass the mind through praise beyond concepts and objective words to more permanently turn it to the positive things of God.

We understand that praise and thanks stir up the power of the Spirit, who is the ultimate instrument of God's grace. We also understand that spoken words have the power to confirm and strengthen thoughts and emotions. So we intentionally allow ourselves to speak praise and thanks beyond objective understanding and words to stir up the Spirit, who can cleanse our thoughts and emotions from negativity more completely than we can.

We do not always praise God because things are going well. Similarly, we do not always pray in tongues because we feel some extraordinary anointing of the Spirit. It is great when it happens, but it does not always happen. Sometimes we pray in tongues by discipline. We do so by choice, as an act of will and faith.

Charismatic signs cannot be manipulated. They are gifts from God that can only be fully received when they are used. Many people say that they will do anything for God *except* speak in tongues. They are unwilling to totally let go of themselves. This is a subtle form of pride. As soon as *except* becomes acceptable in our language with God, God's work in our life is immediately limited.

To receive the gift of tongues we must be willing to open our mouths and verbalize something beyond known language and human logic. Until then, it simply will not happen. Once that attitude of openness is present in our spiritual lives, then we are free to receive all the gifts God chooses to give us. As St. Paul says, some are given this gift, but others are not. To fully receive the gifts in store for us, we must begin by being humble enough to recognize our need for God's gifts in the first place. Unless that happens, we remain stuck in the delusion of pride.

Have you really opened your life to charismatic praise and worship with humility, or are you hanging on to pride and resistance?

Breath Prayer

When the Lord created Adam, he only became a living being when the Lord breathed life into him. When the dry bones were raised up in Ezekiel, they only became living beings when flesh and blood were added to the bones, and God breathed life into the bodies to bring revival. When Jesus gave the Holy Spirit to the apostles before his ascension, he did so by breathing on them.

The Hebrew and Greek words for *spirit* (*ruah* and *pneuma*, respectively) mean "air," "wind," and "breath," specifically the breath of a rational creature. It is appropriate to incorporate the breath with Spirit-led prayer.

It is also an ancient part of Christian tradition. Specifically, breathing is used with the Jesus Prayer. But we can prepare for the Jesus Prayer by learning how to cleanse and quiet our whole being in the Spirit. We bring every part of the old self to the Cross so the new creation can be reborn in Christ through the Spirit. We do this by using the breath with each part of who we are.

We start by breathing in and asking ourselves how our bodily senses are today. Are they healthy or sick? In pain and stiff? In ease and comfort? There are no right or wrong answers here. We simply become aware of how we are doing. Then we breathe out our senses and let them go to God through the Cross of Jesus Christ. We release the senses of our body through the Cross so they can find their right place through his Resurrection.

Then we move to the emotions with the same process. We breathe in and ask ourselves how our emotions are today. Are they agitated or peaceful? Happy or sad? Depressed or hopeful? Then we breathe out and let our emotions go completely though the Cross of Jesus. Only then can they be reborn in their right place.

Lastly, we breathe in our thoughts. How are they today? Are they confused and muddy? Focused and clear? Are they sharp or dull? Again, there are no right or wrong answers. We simply acknowledge how we are. Then we breathe out and let them go completely through the Cross of Jesus. Only when we release all our thoughts, opinions, agendas, and ideas can our thoughts be resurrected in the real mind of Jesus Christ.

When we do this with the old self, our spirit emerges in the Holy Spirit. Our spirit then becomes the primary faculty of our being and the spiritual mind of the soul. The senses, emotions, and thoughts of the mind all find their right place. Thoughts are focused on the spirit in his Spirit, emotions empower us and give us enthusiasm for the things of the Spirit, and the body becomes the vehicle in which this spiritual life unfolds.

Pruning and Ascetical Disciplines

Monastics and all serious followers of Jesus practice asceticism and discipline. Without it they are lost. Such practices are best done under the guidance of a spiritual father or mother, an elder, or a spiritual director.

Asceticism and disciplines such as fasting, vigils, and spiritual reading prune the wild growth from our life. Plants, vines, and trees must be pruned to be fully fruitful and safe. This is also true of the spiritual life.

I remember a big mulberry tree by a farmhouse in Indiana. It was my favorite tree on the farm. We had an old tire swing suspended from one of its larger lower branches. I would spend hours swinging under that majestic tree and looking up at its mighty branches. But its upper branches hung over the top of the farmhouse and were threatening the safety of the house. So we brought in the tree specialists to prune it. I thought they would trim back a few branches and leave the rest.

I was mistaken. After the specialists left, I went out to look at the big tree. Instead of the once-majestic mulberry tree, I saw a nearly naked main trunk with a few scrawny limbs and branches at the top. I was stunned. I was sure that they had killed my favorite tree. But I was mistaken once more. Within two years the tree grew back fuller and more majestic than ever before.

The same happens with plants in the garden. I recall pruning tomato plants. Between each two fruitful branches grows a sucker branch that will never flower and produce tomatoes. It has to be pruned for the plant to produce to its fullest. You pinch the sucker branch with your fingers when it just starts to grow. If you wait too long, the useless branch grows big enough that you must use a small shear.

It is similar when you prune a vine. Of the plentiful green growth, some will bear fruit and some won't. The unfruitful branches must be pruned to allow more nutrients to be sent to the fruitful branches. It is easy to prune visibly dead branches. It is much more difficult to prune the living, but unfruitful, branches. But they will never bear fruit, so it must be done. If we do it when the branches are young, it is relatively easy. If we wait until they are older, it is more difficult; it requires greater effort and special tools.

The same is true with spiritual life. Asceticism and discipline help cut back what is dead in us, but also the wild and fruitless growth. Fasting helps us control the stomach. If we cannot control the most basic things such as the stomach, we cannot control the bigger desires of the flesh.

Vigils help us control the tendency of the flesh toward inordinate sleep and laziness. If we cannot rise a bit earlier for prayer during the quietest times of the night and early morning, we may also find it difficult to have fruitful prayer at other times.

The stages of *lectio divina*, or "spiritual reading"—reading, meditation, prayer, and contemplation—help control and direct the mind to the beautiful things of God. We are what we think, and the battle for the soul is fought in the mind. The mind directs the emotions and the senses. Cultivating the soul is best accomplished by a schedule that ensures that we allot time daily for spiritual reading. If we cannot do this, then the mind tends to wander, the emotions run wild, and the senses eventually rule. That is how we lose the battle for the soul.

There are other disciplines. Which ones are yours? They all help us prune the vine of our spiritual life so that we can bear the fruit of the Spirit in our life. But we should let Jesus prune us as well. Jesus is the vine, and we are the branches.

He prunes the vines he loves so that we will bear abundant spiritual fruit in Christ.

The Spiral Staircase

Spiritual life is like going up or down a spiral staircase.

Western philosophy and religion view time as a linear motion, moving from one point to another, like a line. Eastern philosophy and religion view time as cyclic, going around and around without beginning or end, each round bringing new learning.

Pope Benedict XVI said that neither image is fully complete. He said that spiritual life is more like a corkscrew turned on its side. It moves around and around and moves from one point to another.

I like a similar analogy of a spiral staircase. It goes up or down when viewed from the side. But when viewed from the top, it seems to go around and around within the same space. What makes the difference is which way we are moving, up or down.

St. Peter Damien, the great Camaldolese cardinal and archbishop, said that in our spiritual lives we either go up or down. There is no standing still in Christ. If we try to stay the same—if we try to coast—we go down. In the spiritual life we are either going toward heaven or hell. There is no middle ground.

In spiritual life, it often seems that we face the same issues over and over again. But this does not mean that we aren't going anywhere. It just means that each time we face something similar to what we have faced before, we have a choice. We can either go up or down. So we should be encouraged. Each time we face an issue, we are moving on the staircase to God. But we must make sure we are going up and not down!

The Pebble in the Shoe

The word *scrupulous* comes from the Latin *scrupulus*, a variant of *scrupus*, literally "rough pebble." Scrupulosity is like getting a pebble in your sandal or shoe.

After gaining some insight into sacred stillness and watchfulness, it is common to fall into the trap of scrupulosity. Scrupulosity gets us obsessed about the details of the spiritual life and distracts us from the bigger picture and greater flow. We miss the proverbial forest for the trees. It is the religious version of suffering from obsessive-compulsive disorder!

I often get pebbles in my sandals from the gravel outside of my hermitage in Arkansas. When that happens I cannot walk comfortably. I have to stop and shake the pebble from my sandal before I can walk comfortably up to the monastery for prayers or to community and ministry meetings.

The same holds true in the spiritual life. We often pick up pebbles in our shoes that make it difficult to walk gracefully in Christ and the Church. The pebbles, or details of spiritual life, are real, and serve an important purpose when kept in the right place. But when they get into our sandals or shoes, when minor details become our major focus and preoccupation, they inhibit us from moving gracefully and smoothly through the steps and stages of spiritual life. When we major on the minors, we lose the more important reasons for spiritual life. Instead, we should major on the majors, and minor on the minors.

Do we allow pebbles to keep us from walking gracefully in the Spirit? We shouldn't. But when it happens, don't panic. That would also be scrupulosity. Instead, calmly stop, shake the pebble from your shoe, and walk forward in Christ.

Scrupulosity and Driving between the Lines

Scrupulosity can be likened to obsessive driving.

When we drive, we watch the lines for our lane but we don't obsess about them. If we obsess about each repeating line, we get nervous and begin to jerk the car back and forth. We make our passengers nauseous, and our vehicle becomes a potential hazard.

To drive gracefully, we must look out at an even eye level toward where we want to go. We do not obsess about the lines on the right or left, but we are aware of them. When we focus on the long haul, we almost automatically stay between the lines, and we drive with smoothness and grace.

The same is true in spiritual life. When we obsess about the details of discipline and asceticism, we get nervous and begin jerking back and forth between the lines. All the gracefulness is gone. Our obsessive behavior makes those around us sick, and our life becomes an accident waiting to happen. Often we emotionally and spiritually crash, sometimes injuring ourselves and those we travel with.

In the spiritual life, we focus on the big picture. We gaze out evenly and comfortably to our Destination. We are aware of the details of our spiritual and communal disciplines, but we don't obsess about them. By focusing entirely on Jesus, we almost automatically fulfill the details of our spiritual lives with grace and ease.

If you find yourself obsessing about the lines in the road, don't panic. Just relax and look out evenly at eye level to the road ahead. You will almost automatically stay between the lines and arrive safely and gracefully at your destination.

Come to the Quiet

After the initial success of *The Lord's Supper* in 1978, I built a hermitage with my own hands by a creek in the woods at Alverna Franciscan Center in Indianapolis. It was a lovely oasis in the growing city.

While in the hermitage, I began composing music for the psalms of the Liturgy of the Hours. The music wasn't congregational, or choral like *The Lord's Supper*; it was solitary, quiet, and meditative. I had to let go of almost all my natural training to compose and perform this music. Instead of the more brash steel-string guitar, I played a classical guitar for the first time. Instead of a bolder prophetic stance, I took a more humble and quiet one. Instead of a full chorus and large orchestra, I played alone, adding only a small quartet, harp, and woodwinds. I called the project *Come to the Quiet*.

When I first brought it to the record company, they objected. They said that it was *too* quiet. They said that there was "too much space in it." But they agreed to release it because I had just had a hit record with *The Lord's Supper*. They figured that they could lose a little money after making so much with my previous hit. Well, *Come to the Quiet* sold three times more than *The Lord's Supper*! It shows us that when we let go of old patterns, God often surprises us with his patterns!

Quiet developed as a spiritual discipline in monasticism. In the Christian East, they call it *hesychia,* or "sacred stillness." It involves quieting the body through prayer posture and breath, quieting the mind through fixed and simple meditation, and quieting the emotions, which follow the mind. Then the spirit can emerge in his Spirit.

This is not quietism, which in its worst expression places quiet above all positive teaching and can reject sound doctrine in favor of quiet alone. Authentic Christian quiet builds on positive doctrine: it confirms it, rises above it, and returns to it in the phenomenal world.

But genuine quiet is not something that ordinarily happens automatically, though we have moments that break through to such sacred stillness and quiet. We have to come to the quiet. We have to embark on a journey.

We do this by creating times and places of solitude and silence. Most people do it by finding times and spaces in their homes, parishes, and even workplaces to be alone with the Alone. I did it by moving into a hermitage and the monastery that grew around it. This takes discipline and commitment.

This process usually takes some initial training under teachers. After that, a monastic must commit to a few hours of daily study and prayer and a disciplined life to maintain it. For those living active lives in the world, it takes twenty to thirty minutes once or twice daily, and a disciplined use of the senses, the mind, and the emotions.

As with all discipline and commitment, we are tempted at times to abandon our journey and return to the Egypt of our more noisy and secular world. We really have to make a continual effort to come to the quiet.

Cups in the Rain

Many people wonder about forgiveness and repentance. Sometimes scripture seems to indicate that forgiveness is dependent on repentance. Sometimes we hear people say that love is unconditional and therefore forgiveness is as well. Both understandings are incomplete. The first can lead to legalism that leads to judgmentalism, for no one can fully repent of every sin as perceived by others. The second can lead to a false forgiveness that enables sin. I found the following analogy helpful.

Forgiveness in God is like a beautiful rain of mercy that falls constantly from heaven. We are like cups left out in the yard. The problem is that we have been turned upside down, and therefore cannot collect the rain. It is constantly falling all around us, but we cannot collect the waters of God's mercy. To actually collect the forgiveness of God we must turn ourselves around, right side up. *Repentance* simply means "to turn around." When we repent, it is like turning our cup right side up to collect the forgiveness of God.

Using this analogy, forgiveness is constant and unconditional. However, our ability to benefit from that forgiveness *is* conditional. It depends on whether our cup is right side up. Forgiveness is constant. Repentance activates forgiveness in our personal lives.

Of course, it is important to remember that we cannot repent unless the grace of God is already at work in our lives. But that initial repentance is only the first step. Being filled with the waters of God's forgiveness and mercy takes the rest of our lives in Christ.

St. Francis of Assisi said that those who have fallen into sin should be called back to mercy and forgiveness simply by looking into our eyes. If our eyes are filled with judgment of their sins, they may be repulsed and turn further away. If our eyes are filled with mercy and love, they will be attracted more and more to the forgiveness and mercy of God.

Do we sometimes expect the fullness of forgiveness without repentance? Do we sometimes look upon others with eyes of judgment rather than mercy? Let's make sure that we turn the cups of our own lives toward the constantly falling mercy and forgiveness of God's love in Jesus Christ.

The Still Pond

I can remember lying on a green lawn on a gentle hillside above Lake Wawasee in northern Indiana as a young Methodist boy on a youth fellowship trip. I also remember the small pond at our house in Oklahoma City when I was quite young. Water has always settled my soul and stilled my mind. It seems to set the stage for spiritual life.

I have found a number of good analogies for the spiritual life in Christ and the Church using water. The mystics of the Church would agree.

Sacred stillness, or what the Eastern Christian mystics call *hesychia*, is like a still pond. The pond of our soul is often agitated. The waters are muddied, and we cannot see what lies below the surface of our being. The surface is also choppy and can only reflect a fractured image and likeness of God or creation.

We must become still to let the waters settle. The mud and silt of the constant activity of life, and the dirt of sin, settle to the bottom. The water clarifies. It becomes pure. Then we can see what really lies in the pond of the soul. The surface becomes like a mirror that can rightly reflect the image and likeness of God.

But this is only the beginning—not the end.

Once this occurs, we more clearly see the garbage in our soul. It has been thrown in from daily life and has settled in the deepest part of our soul. We do not leave it there, unforgotten. Instead, we must reach in and pull out the trash. This unsettles the waters once more. We can usually only pull out one or two things at a time. Then we must wait for the waters to settle again before we can pull out some more. This often takes a long time.

Once we remove the garbage that has settled in our life, the waters of the pond become crystal clear, and we reflect God's image beautifully once more.

The Spider and the Web

Sacred stillness is like a spider and a web.

A spider spins its web with much activity. It is hard work and takes much time, but it is worth it. Afterward, the spider waits in perfect stillness so that when something flies into the web, it can sense it at once. The spider then goes out onto the web to find its nourishment. It might be food, or it might be an enemy. The spider can respond accordingly. But it must first do the work of spinning the web, and then be perfectly still.

It is the same with sacred stillness. We must first engage in the active life of overcoming vice and establishing virtue through discipline. Then we can rest and become perfectly still in body, thought, and emotion. Only then can we really sense a disturbance in the web of our life. Once we sense it, we can discern what the disturbance is. It might be healthy spiritual food, or it might be something not nourishing or even dangerous. If it is healthy spiritual food, we are fed. If it is an enemy, we can engage in appropriate spiritual battle.

Are we battling appropriately with what keeps us from him? And then are we resting in him so as to better understand the very web of our life in him?

The Reservoir

St. Bernard of Clairvaux said that contemplative life is like a reservoir. The creek of our life might be quite small. It can be very shallow. At times it might be barely flowing. Sometimes it dries up for weeks and months at a time, and we barely notice it. It affects very little.

But if we damn up that little creek, it becomes a large lake. It becomes a reservoir. It has water to spare in dry times. The reservoir might appear to be still and calm, but there is incredible kinetic energy that builds up deep within it, waiting to be released with new power.

Creatures such as fish, turtles, and even a few snakes all find a home there. Creatures of the land find refreshment there; they drink from the stream with delight. It becomes a hub for all life around it.

Contemplative life can appear to stop the creek, but it actually restores it. It deepens it. It builds its kinetic energy. Contemplation seems to be doing nothing, but it makes the creek into something more. It becomes a large reservoir. It becomes a great lake. Rather than depleting the energy of life, divine energy is stored within it under what looks like stillness. Life flourishes within its still waters, both shallow and deep, and around it. All creatures gather around it to drink. It is only when our reservoir substantially emerges in our life are we able to fully bring this water of life in Christ to others.

Do we take time for retreat and contemplation to build up our spiritual reservoir in Christ?

The Aqueduct

St. Dominic said that apostolic life is not only like a reservoir. It is also like an aqueduct. The reservoir builds the energy, and the aqueduct channels it in a constructive way to bring life to others.

The spiritual aqueduct takes the water of the Holy Spirit built up in the reservoir of contemplative life and channels it to bring water to many more in dry places. It takes the divine energy that has built up by damming the little creek of ordinary prayer life and releases it on a gentle downhill grade to bring water to countryside and city alike.

The aqueduct releases the pressure of the water in a healthy way and keeps the dam from breaking. A dam break can be destructive. Water released in an undisciplined way can destroy the spiritual towns and villages of ordinary life. The release must be disciplined, gradual, and gentle. Then people can dip into it and collect life-giving water for their families and homes.

An aqueduct channels water without keeping any water for itself. In doing so, it serves its divine purpose and discovers what it really is.

The aqueduct must be clean and pure. It cannot pollute the water it channels.

It must be watertight and cannot leak water prematurely. That would leave little water for the destination for which it is intended. It would defeat its own purpose.

So it is with the apostolic life of ministry to others. We must first gather the spiritual water and divine energy in contemplation before we have enough water and energy to spare. Contemplation must precede action, and prayer must precede ministry.

We must channel the water of the Gospel to the dry places of secular life where people are dying of thirst. We must dare go away from the watered gardens around the reservoir and venture into the deserts of modern life.

We cannot keep any of the water for ourselves; we must channel it all for others. We cannot be selfish in our ministry. It is all for others. Our time to be a reservoir was before. In ministry, our water is all for others. Yet in ministering to others we are ministered to ourselves. Only then do we fulfill our purpose and find out who we really are in Christ, who died so that others might truly live.

We must be righteous and pure to minister to others. We must practice what we preach, or our preaching is powerless and vain. We cannot give what we do not possess. If we attempt to do that, we pollute our ministry, and even though it may be successful in the short term, it will eventually fall under the shame of scandal and sin.

We must be watertight so as to bring the water of the Gospel of Jesus Christ to those whom God sent us. We must not leak our ministry ineffectively. We must know our mission and not get sidetracked into other good ministries to which God never called us.

We are aqueducts of God's grace. Are we bringing the contemplative water of the reservoir to all those thirsting for living water in the spirit of Christ?

The Oasis and Canteens in the Desert

The balance between contemplative community and action and ministry is also like providing water in the desert.

Contemplative community life is like an oasis in the desert. The oasis is a center for green, lush life in the Spirit. It is a stopping place for world-weary travelers. Some live there permanently to ensure that the oasis is well cared for. Others stop there frequently on their travels through the desert. But other travelers are stranded and dying of thirst out in the barren desert. Their canteens of water have run dry, and they are too far out to make it back to the oasis on their own. We fill our canteens and venture out to bring them water. We hope to bring them back to the oasis, where we can all drink the life-giving water to our hearts' content.

So we set out. We find a group of stranded, thirsty travelers. We give them water to drink, but we must be careful to save enough for our journey back to the oasis. But some are not careful. Sometimes we see another group close by. They are near death. We hesitate, knowing we must have enough to get everyone back to the oasis, but eventually decide to take a chance. We bring water to them as well. But then we see another group, and then another. In our haste and concern we try to bring water to everyone in one journey.

Suddenly we realize that we have used up almost all the water. There is not enough for such a large group on the journey back to the oasis. We are faced with the probability of certain death of everyone. This is like ministry burnout. It happens to many well-intentioned ministers of the Gospel. The corpses of burned-out ministers litter the spiritual graveyards of the Church.

We must learn to bring water to one or, at most, two groups at a time. We must bring each one back to the oasis, and then set out again until all have been saved. Each time we return, we must fill our canteens so that we have the strength to help more stranded, thirsty travelers. It takes longer, indeed a lifetime. But it can be done. And it saves more lives.

This is like the balance of contemplative community and apostolic ministry. We must be filled from the well of contemplative community before we go out to help others through ministry. Our own spiritual canteens must be full before we can bring spiritual water to others. We must know the path of teaching and practice in community and ministry for the journey so we do not get lost along the way. And we must not get so obsessed with ministry, going frenetically from one project to another, that we run out of spiritual water and lose everyone to thirst in the desert. Then all is lost.

We must learn how to balance sustaining our own lives at the oasis with filling up our canteens and going out to the desert to help those thirsting for God.

Work and Miracles

The balance between ordinary hard work and miracles is like Jesus turning water into wine at the first miracle at Cana.

The story is well known. The events are simple. Jesus goes with his mother to a wedding at nearby Cana. It is probably the house of a relative or friend. In the course of the banquet, they run out of wine. Mary intercedes with Jesus. She knows he has the power to work a miracle, even though his ministry has not yet begun. I imagine that Jesus is hesitant, but his mother has asked, so he acquiesces.

Jesus first tells the servers to bring water. They haul the large containers down to the well, fill them, and lug them back to the house in the hot Middle Eastern sun. It was hard work! Only then does he work a miracle and turn the water into wine. The servers exclaim that usually the best wine is served first, and the lesser quality is served later, but Jesus has saved the best wine for last!

This is like life in the Church. We often run out of the resources we need for spiritual life and ministry. Mary, who typifies the Church, asks Jesus to work a miracle, too. But instead of working an immediate miracle, Jesus asks us to haul some water. It is ordinary hard work! There isn't anything miraculous about it. Only when we have the faith to haul the water does he miraculously turn our water into the finest wine!

The Tension in the Bowstring

The Desert Fathers teach that spiritual life is like a bow and a string. If there is no tension on the bow, it cannot fulfill its purpose of shooting an arrow. If there is too much tension, the bow will snap. There must be tension on the bow and the string, but not too much.

In our spiritual life, we must also have times when we take the string off the bow altogether. These are times for rest and relaxation. Without completely releasing the tension of the string from the bow at times, the bow will snap and will no longer be able to function.

Are we comfortable with the tension on the string? Do we take times for rest and relaxation in our spiritual life?

The Wheat and the Dough

The Old English word for *Lord* means "keeper of the bread." As our Lord, Jesus is making a loaf of supernatural bread from the natural wheat of our lives. Let's apply the natural process of harvesting wheat and making bread to our spiritual lives in Christ.

Wheat must be cut down at the base of the stalk to get to the grains of wheat. Likewise, our natural lives and gifts must be cut down at the base to get to the substance of who we are.

Then the wheat grain must be separated from the plants by gathering the stalks into groups and threshing them against the floor. Likewise, we must be gathered into community in which we face the trials and struggles of life together.

Next, the wheat is winnowed by throwing it into the air on a windy day. The wind separates the wheat grain from the chaff husks, blowing the chaff away and allowing the wheat to fall to the floor. Likewise, we must allow our lives to be thrown up into the air, so the wind of the Holy Spirit can separate the wheat from the chaff of our lives.

The wheat grain must then be ground into flour. We, too, must be ground by the heavy trials of life. Then we end up as good flour to be used for baking the bread of life in our lives.

Water and yeast are added to the flour, and the combination is mixed thoroughly into dough. The yeast is the new life of the Gospel. The water is the gentle, deeper work of the Spirit. We must let God add the grace we need and mix us up from our typical routines, the patterns and ruts that haven't really worked.

The living action of the yeast causes our spiritual dough to rise up in the Resurrection of Christ. In baking, this process is interrupted three times. Just as a baker "punches down" the dough to release excess air, God "pokes" us to get the trapped "hot air" out of our lives. We are all a bit filled with the hot air of ego, and we fall flat each of the three times this is done. Only after the hot air of ego is substantially out of our lives can we be put into the oven and baked into bread.

Finally, we are put into the oven that blazes with the hotter trials of life. But if we relax and allow God to bake us all the way through, we come out as a beautiful brown loaf of heavenly bread in Christ, able to feed the hungry of this world.

This process takes us through a repeated cycle of cross, resurrection, ascension, and empowerment of the Holy Spirit. If we allow it to repeat throughout our lives, then God eventually turns us into his bread. But we must allow the process to play out. We must be patient and trustingly obedient to become his miracle.

Do we submit to going through this process fully? Do we really allow Jesus to be the Lord, or keeper of the bread, in our lives?

Yeast or Alternative Dough

The Gospel is like yeast in the dough; it keeps the entire loaf from falling flat. But it is also an alternative to the dough of the secular world.

Yeast is a very small part of the ingredients needed for making bread. But it is powerful enough to keep all the dough from falling flat in the baking process.

The Church is a very small part of the world, but it is powerful enough to keep the world from self-destruction. One scholar said that it only takes twelve enlightened people on the planet to keep us from destroying each other. It only took twelve apostles to spread the Gospel of Jesus Christ throughout the entire world.

We see this today in the presence of loving and joyful Christians in a world filled with self-absorption and hateful anger. They minister simply by their presence in the world. And the Church, speaking justice and peace to modern issues on cultural and political levels, serves as a conscience for all humanity. It keeps the moral compass of the modern world from going unchecked on a destructive course based on human knowledge alone.

There are communities within the Church that provide an alternative dough alongside the dough of society. Monastic communities are largely self-supporting entities. Throughout history, they have often produced most of what they need to live from within the monastery itself. They often employ hundreds and even thousands of workers to keep their ministries and industries functioning. These alternative communities are a huge inspiration to the secular world, though they often puzzle the secular world as well. This inspiration has special significance in today's world where so much of our secular culture is polluted by rampant sin, and so much of our sin has polluted the earth itself.

Our integrated monastic community at Little Portion is a bit of both models. At the monastery we produce much of what we use in a way that is environmentally responsible and sustainable. But we cannot produce everything, so we must interact with modern society as well. Our domestics try to live simply as well, but they work secular jobs and raise families in which children learn to function in the modern world.

Are we really yeast in the modern world, or are we still unleavened by the Gospel of Jesus and the power of the Holy Spirit? Are we willing to be part of an alternative loaf to the tainted loaf of the modern secular world? We must be a bit of both to be effective witnesses to our faith today.

The Fire of God

God is often described as a holy fire. He was fire in the burning bush, and with the giving of the Law. He was in the pillar of fire at night that led the Israelites out of Egypt, and in the Cloud of the Transfiguration on Mt. Tabor. He was fire at the outpouring of the Holy Spirit at Pentecost in the Upper Room.

Theologians and mystics say that the fire of God is constant. It is our relationship with the Divine Fire that makes the difference in how we experience it. Those who resist find the Fire frightening and hurtful. Those who embrace the Fire find it warming and comforting.

I have spent hours building fires. When I did it rightly in my hermitage in the Indiana woods at Alverna Franciscan Center, I stayed cozy and warm. When I did it badly, I would often awaken with my beard and moustache frozen solid. It took some time to get the hang of it. To this day I thoroughly enjoy building and sitting around a warm fire. It soothes my soul.

There are stages in building a good fire, just as there are in building a good spiritual life. First you gather kindling, or small pieces of dry wood. It must be placed in a fireplace, woodstove, or fire pit. A fire that is not contained can be destructive. The kindling is lit from without. After the fire catches, you use your breath or a bellows to blow air onto the fire to get it burning well.

This is like the fire of God in spiritual life. You start with kindling, or the little things of life. These are the objective teachings of the Church in doctrine regarding faith and morality, and the disciplines of study, prayer, and mortification. These things do not seem like much when compared to the mystical fire of God, but they are essential to get the fire going rightly.

We practice our spiritual lives within the containment of the Church through right worship, teaching, and service. We do so under the guidance of a good pastor, spiritual director, elder, spiritual father, or spiritual mother. We do so in a community or movement that is based on time-tested teachings and practice. To venture outside of these things is to risk building a fire that could become destructive and wild, and burn the whole house down.

The spark must come from without. The kindling cannot make fire by itself. We must use a spark or a match to get the fire going. It is likewise in spiritual life. We have no power in ourselves to create that spark. The fire of God comes from the fire of the Holy Spirit. It exists in us as God's gift, and because we are created in God's image and likeness. Even when we lose his likeness through sin, the image we bear ignites a desire for God and the things of God. Then the Holy Spirit touches the seeking soul with a spark of divine grace that completes our natural longing for goodness, truth, beauty, and love.

Once the fire catches in our lives, we need the wind, or breath of the Holy Spirit, to keep the fire of God going. Without the Spirit, the fire of God will go out. It needs air. It needs the Spirit. Sometimes that breath of the Spirit is kept going with bellows. We use the tools of the Church—sacraments, liturgy, scripture—and the mystical life—asceticism, prayer, apostolic service. If we try to continually blow on the fire ourselves, we might hyperventilate and pass out. We use the right tools for the right job.

But after we get the fire burning, it grows into a raging fire. It is impressive and awe inspiring. But unless it settles into a steady fire, it will take warm air out of the house. Still, the raging fire is essential to get a steady fire going.

This is like the charismatic part of our spiritual life in Christ. Praise and worship of this kind is simply awesome. It is unmatched by the little and comparatively unimpressive fire of the kindling phase. It is emotional, and it lifts us up out of ourselves for God. We are lifted above the inhibitions that keep us from giving ourselves fully to God. In return, we find out who we really are, and we discover a holiness that surpasses all that comes from externals alone. Anyone who has experienced it knows its power, and those who have not yet done so cannot know what it really is.

The raptures of mystical life are similar. They are awesome, even overwhelming. When we are rapt, we are snatched up out of ourselves. We rise above all that we have ever been before, whether in secular or religious life. The natural is surpassed by the supernatural.

But these more passionate experiences and expressions of God's fiery love cannot sustain themselves constantly. In fact, just as the raging fire takes heat out of the house, these raptures of mystical life can actually drain us of our energy in God if we constantly seek to stir them up as our only experiences and expressions of our love for God.

After the raging fire is established for a while, the wood becomes hot coals and embers that burn steadily. They heat the house. They aren't as impressive as the raging fire, but they do more good. And they are quite relaxing to sit beside on a cold winter's night.

This is like the contemplative stage in our life with Christ. After the charismatic stage, we enter contemplation almost naturally. The awesome experiences give way to simply *being* with the One Who *Is*. It is not externally impressive; there are no external aids like spiritual kindling or bellows applied anymore. Some may not even recognize what they are experiencing. But it heats the house of the soul more effectively. It does more good for us and for others.

This final contemplative stage, however, usually cannot be entered into unless we go through the previous stages first. We cannot have the hot coals without the raging fire, and we cannot have the raging fire without the kindling. And here's the trick for a skilled fire starter: If the coals have been built up properly, there are still embers left in the fireplace the next morning. From those embers the process may be started again for the following day.

Spiritual life does not progress from one stage to another, with any one stage never to be repeated again. We go through the stages over and over again all through our lives. We go from mystical sparks to the kindling of external disciplines and doctrines. We go from external doctrine and disciplines to the roaring fire of charismatic experiences and mystical raptures. Then we move from the raging charismatic and mystical fire to the hot coals that really heat the house. We do this repeatedly through life at various times and seasons. We do this both personally and communally. The fire of God is not static. It is alive, and it heats the house of the soul, the Church, and the world.

The Water of the Spirit and the Oil of Sin

Righteousness and sin are like oil and water. They do not mix.

Oil rises to the top of water. While they can inhabit the same glass or vessel, sooner or later the water will displace the oil. If we want to displace the oil completely, we must fill the glass completely with water.

In this image, the oil represents sin, and water is like righteousness in the Spirit. Water displaces oil, and righteousness displaces sin. But if we want to eliminate the oil from our lives, we must allow ourselves to be filled to the brim with the Holy Spirit. The living water of the Holy Spirit naturally removes the oil of sin. It raises sin to the top of our lives where it can be removed.

If we want to stop doing the don'ts, we must get busy and start doing the dos! We cannot do both at the same time. Good thoughts displace bad thoughts. Good emotions displace bad emotions. And good actions displace bad ones.

The water of the Spirit displaces the oil of sin. While we may temporarily have both within us, the water of the Spirit eventually removes all the oil of sin from our lives. But it takes a little time.

Water in a Clean, Empty Vessel

Life in the Spirit is also like water in an empty, cleansed vessel. This can happen in two ways.

First, we can pour the water into the vessel, displacing whatever liquid was in the vessel beforehand. The problem is that it does not always sufficiently cleanse the vessel, and that leaves the water inside the vessel impure.

Second, we can empty the vessel of the old liquid first. Then the vessel can be cleansed before the pure water is poured into it.

This is like life in the Spirit. Yes, the Spirit can displace the liquid of our old selves, but we remain dirty from the residue of our old lives of sin. So it is sometimes better to empty ourselves of our old selves first. Then it is possible to cleanse the residue of our old selves of sin through prayer and virtue. Then we can be filled to the brim with the purity of the Holy Spirit. In monastic life, this is the way of the great elders who are reverently called "Spirit bearers."

Emptying yourself from the old self is accomplished through prayer, asceticism, and virtue. But even with the second way, it is important to remember that the life of prayer, asceticism, and virtue cannot be accomplished without the grace of the Holy Spirit in the first place. Doing these things on your own power is ultimately futile, and results in great religious frustration.

Conversely, not using any human effort at all—waiting for the Spirit to do everything—also results in frustration. God wants a love relationship with us, a relationship of cooperation with grace. In such a relationship God leads, and we must do the work of following him.

Are we letting go of the old self to the Cross of Jesus Christ so that we can be born again day by day, minute by minute, and even moment by moment through the grace of the Holy Spirit in our life?

Are we embracing the healthy disciplines of prayer, asceticism, and virtue so that the Spirit can fill us to the brim?

Priming the Pump

For a number of years I lived on a small organic farm in Indiana. We had a wonderful old hand pump next to a lovely guesthouse. But at times it ran dry. During those times we had to prime the pump. It taught me an important lesson about dry times in the spiritual life.

Stirring up the Spirit is like priming a pump. When a pump is dry, you pour water down the pump, and then you pump the handle. It seems like the opposite of what you should do. Why waste the little bit of water that remains? But to prime a pump you pour the remaining water down the dry well. And you pump! Soon water flows from deep below and gushes forth in abundance.

The same is true in spiritual life. We all experience times of dryness. We only seem to have a little bit of spiritual water left. It is precisely at that point that we must use that water and pour it down the shaft of our spiritual life. Then we must pump with all the spiritual tools at our command. Soon the water of the Holy Spirit will burst forth.

This is true with both praise and devotions. It is precisely when I feel the least bit inclined to praise God that I must do so. I lift my heart, my voice, and my hands and praise God, even though I don't feel like it! I do so by faith, not by feelings. Soon authentic praise of God and a positive attitude toward everyone and everything wells up from my soul.

We praise God because, as St. Paul writes, we know that all things work together for the good of those who love God. We also thank God everywhere and for everything in our Lord Jesus Christ. We praise God for the many small good things we often take for granted. We also thank him for our difficulties, for these have lessons to teach us about relying on grace when we are humbled and brought low.

The same is true with devotions. For me it is scripture and the Jesus Prayer. I sometimes combine the first part of the Hail Mary with the Jesus Prayer. It is precisely when I don't feel like doing these prayers that I must do so. I sit down, pull out scripture or the Jesus Prayer rope, and I pray. Many folks do the same with the Rosary. Whatever works best for you, use these devotions if they normally bring you closer to Christ. You can amend them, but it is best to do so with the input of your spiritual father or mother, an elder, or a spiritual director. Then you will know that you are not doing so from pride.

What devotions are part of *your* daily life?

PART THREE

The Church

Christ, Christian, and Catholic

I have led seemingly countless retreats at our old Little Portion Retreat and Training Center in Arkansas, and a few elsewhere. I discovered quickly that average Christians often need a foundation from which to present the more detailed content and experience of the retreat. So I usually begin with the basics: Jesus is the Christ. We are Christians. And we are Catholics. Each of the words—*Christ, Christian, Catholic*—has powerful significance that might be surprising.

Christ

In Greek, *Christos*, or *Christ*, simply means "anointed." The Holy Spirit anointed Jesus. Jesus was inspired, inspirited, and inbreathed by the breath of God the Father. In Jesus is the fullness of God—the Father, the Son, and the Holy Spirit—in a perfect communion of love.

Anointing is pouring oil—amply, not a mere smear or smudge—over the head of another. The Bible says it runs over the head and down the beard of Aaron.

Anointing also means to rub oil in deeply. It is like a deep and repeated massage by God. It transforms us.

Anointing occurs at the consecration of new altars. Oil is applied generously and rubbed in deeply. The bishop rubs in the holy oils repeatedly, and not without some joy. And he must wear a liturgical apron! The oil is ample indeed.

Christian

We are Christian, or *Christianos* in Greek. The word *Christian* was first used in Antioch. We are in the intimate company of Christ. What he is by nature, we are by grace. We are anointed with the same Spirit who anointed Jesus Christ. The Spirit anoints us amply, deeply, and repeatedly.

When anointed with the Spirit we become "like Jesus." His Sermon on the Mount becomes our new way of living. The great "love chapter" of St. Paul is our inspiration. We bear the fruit of the Holy Spirit that changes our character and behavior from the inside out. We experience love, joy, peace, patience, mildness, kindness, generosity, chastity, and faith. These are the things we long for. And though we often fall short, these are what we are made for. Without them we are in a constant state of frustration, dogged by a sense of not really knowing who or what we are.

This change is not merely external or brought on by brute force—though it does require a choice and the discipline to persevere. It is an inner impelling that changes us from the inside out. It is Jesus in us being the Christ deep within us. We recognize our deepest selves in the person of Jesus and are empowered by the Holy Spirit to become who we really are—who we were created to be by God. When we hear scripture and his Word, his Spirit within us recognizes himself in them. Until then, we are always empty, always frustrated, and always alone.

Sometimes this empowerment comes like a strong driving wind. Other times it is a gentle breeze or a well springing up from within. The Spirit empowers and impels us in many wonderful ways.

Catholic

We are Catholic, or *Catholicos* in Greek. *Catholic* was first used by St. Ignatius of Antioch. It means "universal and full." We are filled with Jesus from the inside out, and from the outside in. He flows upon us from head to toe and wells up from the deepest spirit inside us. To be Catholic includes a creed and a faith community, but we are far more than a creed. We are filled with Jesus and in common union, or communion, with him as a united people. We are filled with the Father and the Son through the power of the Holy Spirit. Today, let's follow Jesus Christ as Catholic Christians.

The Safety Net and the Trampoline

The Church is like a huge safety net stretched beneath the high-flying acrobats and trapeze artists of a circus. The high-flying artists are the monastic and nonmonastic saints and mystics who reach stunning heights and perform dazzling feats of skill above the rest of us in their relationship with Jesus Christ. We need both the safety net and the high-flying artists for a good circus. The safety net without the trapeze artists is boring. But the trapeze artists who fly without a safety net put their lives at risk.

Likewise with the Church. The safety net is the apostolic succession and the Petrine ministry of the bishops in communion with the successor to St. Peter, the pope. The beautiful balance of sacred tradition and sacred scripture is preserved and taught by the magisterium, the Church's teaching authority. The Church also gives us the sacraments, most especially the Eucharist. The mystics and saints of the Church are best found in the monastic heart of the Church, though there are saints and mystics from every state of life. The safety net is very important! Indeed, we need experts to construct and maintain it. These are the bishops, clergy, and theologians.

Sacred scripture, apostolic tradition, and the sacraments keep us from falling to the hard ground when we fall. It is important to study, build, and maintain a strong and sturdy safety net. But we do not obsess or focus on the safety net. When attending the circus, our attention is drawn to the stunning feats of the high-flying trapeze artists. Similarly, we must focus on the awesome art of the mystics and the saints who inspire us to follow their example of reaching such amazing spiritual heights in following Jesus Christ.

The Church is also like a trampoline. From the elasticity, strength, and power of the trampoline, we are able to reach heights in Christ we could never achieve if trying to do so from the ground alone. We would simply jump up and down in vain. But we do not focus on the trampoline. Rather, we watch the trampoline acrobat. This, too, is like the balance between the Church and the saints.

The Body: Mind, Heart, Skeleton

St. Paul said that we are the Body of Christ, and the Church is like a body.

A body has a mind for thought, a heart for emotions, and a skeleton for structure. A body without a unified mind cannot have direction. Without a heart it has no emotions or motivation. Without a skeleton it is just a blob of flesh, unable to accomplish anything despite the best ideas or emotions.

Likewise with the Church. We must have a unified mind regarding our doctrine, faith, and morality as followers of Jesus. We have unity in diversity. But if we are of many minds, we cannot make up our minds as to what we believe or how we should live.

We must have a heart for devotion, and emotion in our worship and life together as disciples of Jesus. We can have a mind unified in doctrine, but without a heart to inspire us in devotion we remain cold and lifeless.

We must have a skeleton, a unified structure to accomplish the things we think or feel strongly. Without a unified structure, we might want to accomplish something but we are unable to do so. If the bones are disjointed, then each respective member of the Church cannot work in grace-filled harmony with the other members. Everything is tortured and painful. The skeleton of the Church is found universally in the pope, nationally and regionally in each conference and bishop, locally in the clergy, and throughout the Church in the various consecrated communities, spiritual movements, and parishes.

Finally, to be fully alive, we must also have a spirit enlivened by the Holy Spirit of God. But without the body the

Spirit becomes disembodied and unable to accomplish anything in the created world.

The Church has always had schisms and heresies, and those who cause division. Beyond these, some faithful want to focus only on emotions, or the inspirational and devotional aspects of our faith. Others want to focus only on orthodox doctrine and theology. Still others tend to focus on ecclesiology, or the structures of the Church. Understandably, each of us has a unique interest as well as a natural and spiritual gift. But sometimes we try to operate independently of each other. Sometimes we even try to act as though another part is not important. This divides the Church. It keeps us from accomplishing our mission in Christ.

The Church must have a skeletal system, a unified mind, and a devoted heart to be a complete Body of Christ. We must also be empowered by the Holy Spirit. Otherwise we remain divided and incomplete.

Do we settle for a version of the Church that is good but incomplete?

The Rock Wall

I started my religious vocation by building a hermitage by a creek at the old Alverna Retreat Center in Indianapolis. I learned a lot in the Spirit by laying blocks and stones while I prayed.

The Church has traditions, and the Church grows and moves forward. Some of us are so traditional that we do not allow for expansion and growth. Others of us are so interested in growth that we throw out beautiful traditions of our apostolic history in Christ.

The Church is like a rock wall. We are living stones in the spiritual temple of the Holy Spirit. The wall is built on the foundation of the apostles and prophets with Christ Jesus—the Stone the religious builders rejected—as the Cornerstone. Everything fits together in relation to him.

Generation after generation the wall is built on that foundation. One course after the other is laid until it reaches a great height. In this we are appropriately conservative. We must place our stones squarely on top of the solid stones that have come before. If we place our stone too far to the right or the left, the wall will eventually lean and fall. If the wall falls, then our individual stones will shatter on the hard ground.

But we are also progressive. We must place our stones where no stone has gone before. If we try to simply repeat the pattern of the lower stones, we cannot build higher. It is an exercise in frustration. But if we try to place our stone higher in midair, we will fall to the ground again. It must be squarely placed on what has come before.

We conserve the rich traditions that have come before. This is a living principle. We know who our teachers are. Our faith is passed on from the apostles to their successors and from one teacher to another. It is passed on not merely in a book but from life to life. While the book is the earliest written measuring stick of all that comes after, not everything that follows is explicitly contained within it. Apostolic tradition is written and unwritten. It is alive, and it gives life.

While we conserve apostolic tradition, we do not get trapped in vain traditions. Folks like this—trapped in vain tradition—rejected Jesus Christ, the Cornerstone. Vain traditions are a lifeless imitation of what came before. Apostolic tradition, on the other hand, is life giving and creative.

Which sort of tradition are we most anxious to preserve? Are we willing to build the wall higher, or are we stuck in the courses of stones laid long ago? Where are we setting the stones of our lives?

Spokes on the Wheel

The Church is called to address many things, both inside each of us and in the world in which we live. All these issues, whether stemming from so-called conservative or progressive aspects of the Church, flow out of our primary relationship with Jesus Christ.

Conservatives often focus on the role of Mary, the pope, and the Eucharist in our life together. Progressives tend to focus more on social-justice issues. These are the things that get our proverbial spiritual giggle going. While all these things are important in their proper place, our primary focus should be on a *personal encounter with Jesus Christ*. Jesus is the one who we need to be most excited about. Everything else is secondary. This primary spiritual encounter with Christ is personal and empowering.

The same is true of our empowerment by the Holy Spirit. It is through the power of the Spirit that our encounter with Jesus Christ becomes personal. It is through the power of the Holy Spirit that Word, sacrament, and everything else in the Church and in the world truly begins to come to life. Without the power of the Spirit, it all becomes the lifeless religion that Jesus spoke so strongly against.

This is like spokes on a wheel. The hub of the wheel is that personal encounter with Jesus Christ. Spokes point outward from that hub and touch many important theological, ecclesiological, and sociological realities. But when we disconnect the spokes of the wheel from the hub, the wheel cannot properly turn and we get nowhere.

This has happened often in our history and in our modern experience. Progressives and conservatives can become obsessed with their particular issues and miss the more primary personal encounter with Jesus Christ from which all issues flow and are solved.

Are we focusing on the hub or the spokes of our spiritual life in Christ?

Right Foot, Left Foot:
Walking Forward as the Body of Christ

I came into the Catholic Church in 1978, at the height of the charismatic renewal and after the Second Vatican Council. It was an exciting time. Possibility was palpable in the air. Everyone was aware that exciting things were happening. But there were also folks who went too far and advocated a version of the Church that was really less than fully Roman Catholic. They upset traditionalists who were quick to accuse anything but an ultraconservative version of the Church of heresy and schism.

My spiritual father was always big on peaceful balance, but he also knew how to live with creative tension. He knew that our understanding and expressions of faith had developed and would develop even more in the years ahead. He expected that things would shift again. He taught me the following analogy.

The Church is the Body of Christ. As such, she has a left foot and a right foot. The Church must use both feet to go forward. First she walks on one foot, then the other, but she goes forward.

If we try to be perfectly balanced at all times, we cannot walk. We might well be perfectly balanced, but we will never move. To walk we must risk losing our balance temporarily to put one foot forward. But when we do this in succession, we establish a greater balance that moves us forward.

These two feet are like the conservative and progressive aspects of the Body of Christ. First we walk on the progressive foot, and then on the conservative foot. But the Church stays balanced and goes forward.

From the conservative Jewish perspective, the first Christians were progressive. Later generations would have to pull back to a conservative Christian perspective to keep from lapsing into unorthodoxy. It could be said that this was the case with Gnostics, who tried to fit Christ into a pagan paradigm outside of his more Jewish context. Others were too conservative, afraid to move forward or expand their understanding of the faith they had received. It could be said that this was the case with the likes of Arians, who resisted any use of new language to better explain the nature of the Son of God. So it went for generations. It is still going on today.

My spiritual father told me that it would be likely that I would see the Church shift from one foot to the other two or three times in my lifetime. As technology speeds up, it could happen more frequently. Though a generality, when I first became a Catholic, the Church was more on the left foot after Vatican II. Then she came back to the right foot under the latter part of St. John Paul II's pontificate, and under Pope Benedict XVI. Now we are moving back toward the middle with Pope Francis. The future still lies before us.

At any given time, some of the faithful might panic that the Church has become unbalanced. They may even complain. This creative tension is needed to shift from one foot to the other. Dialogue is healthy; even debate can be healthy in a more controlled scholastic forum. But too much tension can be caused by hanging on to one or the other foot, causing us to hop rather than walk gracefully. We must shift from one foot to the other. It can be unnerving at times for all of us, but viewing it from a broader perspective, we will see that all is well. We are moving forward in a straight line. We can be at peace.

Are we comfortable with the tension we feel when the Church alternates between left and right?

Scribes and Pharisees

Jesus loved sinners and was most forgiving of drunks, prostitutes, and tax collectors. But he was most harsh with the religious leaders of his day. They claimed to know God, but they rejected God's Son. They came by many different names and were grouped into different movements. Those mentioned in scripture are the scribes and Pharisees, the Sadducees, and the Zealots.

The scribes were the archconservative keepers of the Law. They were the clerks of the Jewish leaders. They inscribed, or wrote down, and kept the old and new legislation.

The Pharisees were a relatively new progressive reform and renewal group during the time of Jesus. At the same time, they were hyperenthusiasts for the Law and prophets. They revived traditions of the Jewish faith. They also believed in the soul's life after death, the resurrection of the dead, and even in a Messiah who sounded uncannily like Jesus. But they missed love for Jesus in favor of zeal for the Law.

The Sadducees were the ultraconservatives and rationalists of their day. They did not believe in resurrection or a soul that lived on after death. They expected a Messiah who would be earthly and human. They did not believe what they could not see. They rejected Jesus because they considered him too much like the Pharisees, and they considered him a blasphemer.

The Zealots were the political activists of their day. They put their hopes in a Messiah who would restore the political kingdom of Israel. They ultimately did not see much in

Jesus to support, for he spoke of a kingdom that was not of this world.

The scribes and Pharisees, the Sadducees and Zealots, are still with us. They have different names now, but they still persecute Jesus in those who want to follow him authentically. Nothing much has changed except the name of the religion they follow.

My spiritual father told me that God allows the scribes and Pharisees into the Church so that we might experience something of what Jesus experienced in the Jewish religious culture of his time.

Though not exact, let me adapt the analogy. The scribes are the clerical and lay workers of our various dioceses, parishes, and communities. They often are well intentioned, and God knows we need such workers. They are often the voice on the phone in many ministries. At times they can be the voice of God or an angel. But if they obstruct God's work by being too impersonal or busy, they can sound like the voice of a demon. This happens when they lose sight of the heart of ministry in the clerical concerns of their work.

The Pharisees are often found among both the zealous progressives and traditionalists in the Church. But they are frequently more dedicated to progressivism or traditionalism than they are to the real work of the Holy Spirit. They can also be like those who are enthusiastic about what is legal. Not mere legalists, who lack enthusiasm and can be lifeless and cold, these people are genuinely enthusiastic for the laws and rituals of the Church. Sometimes, though, they miss the real work of the Spirit of God. They claim to be progressive and the most informed, but they miss the real Word of God in their midst. They claim to be orthodox but miss authentic worship. They cannot see Jesus due to their obsession with detail and their own agenda for the Church.

The Sadducees are the rationalists and ultraconservatives of the Church. When it comes to theology or liturgy, they accept only the legalistic interpretations of the past. They are all about externals. They cannot accept the supernatural things of the Spirit, because they are stuck in the ruts of the natural. They cannot see miracles, because they cannot see past the mundane. And they always miss Jesus while claiming to be the most obedient to him.

The Zealots are the political activists of the Church. They tend to see Jesus through the matrix of their particular liberal or conservative political perspective. Instead of letting Jesus inform our politics, they remake Jesus according to their own political positions. They still miss Jesus because they are more about politics and power in the temporal world than they are about Christ.

All these groups miss God in the name of God. They try to remake God according to their image and likeness instead of letting God remake them according to his image and likeness. They make a god out of their approach to God. They worship religion but miss Jesus, who is the ultimate reason for religion. They make a god of their form of godliness without understanding the power of the spirit of God.

Truth be known, there is a bit of the scribe, Pharisee, Sadducee, and Zealot in all of us. We must be careful that we don't miss Jesus, too!

Are we today's scribes and Pharisees, Sadducees and Zealots? We might change the names, but we cannot change the spiritual blindness. We must let go of our old religious and political affiliations and categories to really let Jesus open our eyes. Only then will we be able to clearly see with new eyes and be his followers. Only then will we really be Christians.

Apostles and Prophets

The Church is built on the foundation of the apostles and prophets, with Christ Jesus as the cornerstone. They are models and types for clerical and lay ministry.

The apostles represent the clergy. They were the first bishops, and all bishops are successors to the apostles. All priests and deacons receive faculties for ministry from the bishops. They are prefigured in the Jewish faith by the priesthood of Aaron and the Levites.

The prophets in the Jewish faith were not all priests. Likewise, in Christian faith not all prophets have been apostles. In Church history, not all who engaged in a prophetic ministry were bishops, priests, or deacons. Some were laity. Some were monks and nuns, consecrated religious and seculars. Some were men, and some were women.

But apostles, too, can be prophets. Bishops, priests, and deacons can and should speak in prophetic ways to the Church and the world. This is self-evident in the bishops and popes who have challenged the Church and the world.

The Church is a ladder leading from earth to heaven. It is a ladder to God. It has two parallel uprights, the apostolic and the prophetic ministries. But for anyone to climb the ladder, there must be steps at regular intervals keeping the apostolic and the prophetic together.

The Church is also like a cupola. This is represented beautifully in the pillars that support the cupola, high above the altar in St. Peter's in Rome. Running up each pillar are intertwined representations of the apostles and the prophets.

Today we need to respect the apostles in our midst. Our clergy are essential to our Church and must be respected. But we also need to more formally respect the prophets who come from all the states of life in the Church. Most importantly, the apostolic and the prophetic voices need to respect one another. Unless they work together at every step, no one can climb the ladder of the Church to God, and the altar of the Eucharist will not be surrounded by the apostolic and prophetic gifts of God.

The Three-Legged Stool

I come from the evangelical Protestant tradition. As such, I have a great love for scripture. But after a decade or so in the Jesus Movement of the late 1960s and '70s, I found the *sola scriptura*, or scripture-alone tradition, unworkable and indefensible. That prompted me to search for something more. I soon discovered that scripture came from apostolic tradition and that both were united under the Church's teaching authority, or magisterium. Ironically, it was my love for the authority of scripture that led me to the authority of the Catholic Church.

The relationship between sacred scripture, apostolic tradition, and the magisterium of the Church is like a three-legged stool. Stools need at least three legs to stand. One leg is impossible. Two is very difficult; the chair totters back and forth. You need a minimum of three legs for a stool to balance properly. That is why most short stools, such as milking stools, are three-legged.

The same can be said regarding scripture, tradition, and magisterium.

Scripture alone, or *sola scriptura*, will not stand. It totters in its attempt to stand firm, leaning first this way, then another. It struggles at best but almost always falls over completely. Scripture, the earliest written record of apostolic tradition, is the measuring stick by which all further development in the Church is measured. Not everything is explicitly in scripture, but the universal principles of the Gospel are implicitly found there.

Separating scripture from tradition divorces from the Church the scripture that was used by God to write and compile it. It disregards the apostolic life that brought it forth and allows scripture to be interpreted and applied in ways never intended or practiced by the Church. Ultimately it does violence to the scriptures themselves and to the very people they were meant to inspire and guide. This can be seen in the fractures, divisions, and hurtful errors and confusions in the various faith communities and sects inspired by the Protestant Reformation.

Instead, scripture and tradition must be seen together as separate currents of one sacred stream of revelation. This can be seen in both Orthodox and Catholic Christianity.

But scripture and apostolic tradition aren't enough either. The stool sits better on two legs than on one, but it still totters on the verge of falling over completely.

While scripture and tradition together better maintained the orthodoxy of the Early Church, they failed to bring the entire Church together in a unity of diversity. The Church still needs an authority to interpret her teachings. This can be seen in the existing divisions of the Orthodox and Eastern churches, who so often break fellowship with one another, as well as in the divisions of non-Orthodox Christians over doctrinal and liturgical matters. Most of the major heresies in the Early Church came forth from various cities with venerable apostolic tradition and scripture but without the authority to unite the entire Church.

We need the central teaching authority, the magisterium of the Church, to authoritatively interpret and apply the inspiration and guidance found in sacred scripture and apostolic tradition in a way that can unite more than a billion followers of Jesus Christ today. That authority is found in the various sees of ancient apostolic antiquity in full communion with the pope, the bishop of Rome.

The Regathering

I am descended from the founder of many Methodist singing churches on my mother's side. As an adult, after leaving that upbringing and searching world religions, I accepted Jesus in 1971 and got involved in the Jesus Movement. This movement was largely Protestant in its theology.

When I became a Catholic, I was very aware that, despite the fullness of faith in the Catholic Church, my Methodist and Jesus Movement years were also gifts from God. I longed—and still long—to see the best of all Christian faith traditions brought together to do something greater than any have achieved in our culture in this era. As I meditated on scripture, the dispersion and regathering of the Jewish people quickened in my heart and mind as a model for how to do that.

For me, the dispersion and regathering of God's people in the Jewish scriptures prefigures the regathering of God's New Testament people. God established a homeland, the Temple, and a Law for his people. He ordained that homeland and promised to keep them there as long as they were faithful. The Temple was based on a sacrifice and a priesthood ordained by God through the Law. The prophets tell us that the leaders and the people turned away from God. And so, after many warnings, they were scattered from the homeland.

But God still loved his people, so he shepherded them in the dispersion. He raised up the synagogue system and a rabbinical leadership to shepherd his people in the Diaspora. The synagogue was based on a word service, and the rabbis were not priests but men called by God from any tribe. This system lasted for hundreds of years.

Then, through the prophets, God called the people back to the homeland to rebuild the Temple and reestablish the priesthood. So they returned home to the original boundaries of the homeland, Temple, and priesthood ordained by God. But they did not reject the work that God had done over the intervening years. They brought the synagogue system and rabbinical leadership back with them as well and integrated them with the Temple and the priesthood. The Temple was in Jerusalem. The synagogues and rabbis were in most larger villages and cities of Israel.

It is interesting to observe that, historically, not many Jews actually returned home. Many stayed in the Diaspora because they had become very successful in the countries to which they were dispersed. But they often supported those in the homeland with their abundance. It took humility and sacrifice to let go of that success and actually make the journey back home. And it took humility for those who had never left to accept the blessings from those who experienced great success in the Diaspora.

This is all similar to what happened in the orthodox Catholic Church, first with the schism between East and West, and then more clearly with the Protestant Reformation.

God ordained the Catholic Church. God established a leadership, worship, and lifestyle in the bishops as successors to the apostles, and the pope as the successor of Peter. God established the Eucharist and sacraments, and a life of Christlike holiness. But the leaders and the laity sinned and departed from God. So after many calls for reform, God dispersed people from the original homeland of the Catholic Church. He did this first as a warning in the schism between East and West, but without changing anything essential, and then in the Protestant Reformation.

But God still loved his people. So he shepherded them and raised up new leaders in a word-oriented worship we see mainly in the Protestant Reformation. The worship was based more on the scriptures than on the sacrificial nature of the Eucharist. And the leaders were not priests but simply ministers.

Now God is calling his people to regather in his original homeland. That homeland is the Catholic Church. The synagogues are the churches of the Reformation. God wants the Reformation communities to come back home. This takes sacrificing some of their more limited autonomy. But God also wants the Catholic Church to accept the gifts he bestowed on his people in the Reformation. Each must have the humility to learn from the other, without destroying the gift of either.

Just as is recorded in the Old Testament, many will not respond actively to this call for regathering. The various churches and faith communities have often enjoyed much success in their dispersion. They enjoyed God's blessings there. It takes sacrifice to humble ourselves and answer the call. It takes sacrifice. And those who never left must be humble enough to accept the blessings of those who return.

This is from *A Way of Life*, a noncanonical guideline and spirituality for the community I founded, the Brothers and Sisters of Charity:

> *Regathering*: As a Catholic and Christian ecumenical community, we intentionally see the dispersion and regathering of the Jews of the Old Testament as a possible symbol and pattern of our ecumenical mission. As the Jewish people were given a divinely ordained leadership of priests, a lifestyle based on the law, and a worship centered on temple sacrifice, so has the new Israel been given an ordained leadership of apostles and their successors, a lifestyle based on the law of love, and a worship centered on liturgy and sacrament. As the Jewish people were dispersed by God for the sins of the leaders and the people, so has the New Testament church been dispersed for the sins

of both the shepherds and the flock. As God continued to shepherd his people in dispersion by raising up a new rabbinical leadership and a word-oriented worship in the synagogue system, so has God continued to shepherd the people of the New Testament dispersion through various ecclesial communities of the Reformation. Likewise, as God regathered the dispersed Jews of the synagogue and integrated them with the original leadership and worship of the Temple, so must we regather the legitimate leadership and worship gifts of the Reformation and integrate them with the original apostolic leadership and Eucharistic worship of the Catholic Christian expression. We integrate while retaining the legitimate integrity of both. ([Berryville, AK: Brothers and Sisters of Charity, 1985], 32)

The Stream and the Tree

Any casual student of Christian theology and history knows that Church doctrines—how we express the Trinity, truths about Christ, or the Holy Spirit, just to name three—developed over time. Some would say those developments went too far and either overstepped the original understandings of the faith or degenerated them altogether. Others would say that they did not go far enough, that they are stuck in archaic expressions that are no longer relevant.

Bl. John Henry Newman expanded on the teaching of St. Vincent of Lérins and brought us an entire work called *An Essay on the Development of Christian Doctrine*. It is considered a masterpiece and is a foundational work for the inspiration of Vatican Council II. In this master work, he compared the development of Christian doctrine to a creek or tree.

In the beginning of my vocation I had a hermitage in the woods by the creek at Alverna Franciscan Center. I spent weeks of hours meditating on the creek and the trees. My spiritual father had given me a copy of Newman's *An Essay on the Development of Christian Doctrine* and explained the analogies. It took decades to really understand the book, but I understood the analogies right away.

The development of Christian doctrine is like a creek as it advances through the countryside. A creek takes on different appearances as it faces different obstacles, but it is the same water throughout. Sometimes it is choppy, and sometimes placid and still. At times it is almost stagnant, but it also falls downhill in rapids. Sometimes it spreads out in stills that are broad and wide, and other times it is narrow in rapids that are almost violent. It all depends on the obstacles it meets along its banks and in its bed. But it is the same creek throughout.

The water also appears to be different. Sometimes it is crystal clear, and other times muddy. Sometimes it is abundant with algae and weeds that make it impossible to see but a few inches below the surface, and other times only its bed is lined with rocks that enable us to see clear to the bottom. But it is the same water all along.

In the Church, doctrine develops but it does not essentially change. We raise different questions and objections according to the needs of the culture and time, and the answers present different aspects of ancient teaching in seemingly new and different ways. But the doctrine is the same all along. Consequently, teachings that seem primitive or even unclear in scripture develop and become clearer as the Church progresses through time.

The Church is also like a mighty oak tree that grows from a small acorn. The fullness of the mighty oak is present as potential in the acorn but is not yet seen. When you look at the oak and the acorn, you would swear that they are not the same thing. But one grows from the other.

From my hermitage I have watched many small shoots grow into majestic and mighty trees as the years passed in my contemplation. Those that were once small and frail became tall and mighty. This took decades, and when viewed daily very little seemed to change at all. But over time their growth became visible.

It is likewise with the development of doctrine. Scripture and the earliest Church Fathers' writings can seem like acorns compared to the mighty oak of later teaching. One could be tempted to say that they are unrelated. They often look like two different things at any one given period or geographic region in Christian history. But the later development is there as potential in the earlier. The mighty oak is present in the acorn.

It takes some time and patience to see this mystery fully. I have remained still and stable for decades, but much has developed outside. It does not happen overnight or even in a matter of months. It often takes decades to see such development in a tree. With the Church it can take centuries. To understand this mystery we must take a long view of history. We must remain stable and still. We must immerse ourselves in the traditional teaching of saints, mystics, and masters. Then we must watch it develop through the ages and into our own day.

An acorn, however, cannot become a pine, a poplar, or another kind of tree altogether. Nor can the mighty oak revert completely to the acorn. That would be change and degeneration. We want development, but not change or degeneration.

Some try to change the teaching of the Church into something it was never meant to be. Others try to go back to the acorn and ignore the mighty oak as illegitimate. Neither of these is true development of Christian doctrine.

Once we see the beauty of the principle, then everything takes on a wonderful new aspect. Doctrine ceases to be mere legalistic code but becomes a living reality that is sent by the living God to guide his people in every culture, situation, and time. Life becomes an adventure in the living God that is fully rooted in the past but that enthusiastically grows into the future.

The Ship, the Sail, and the Rudder

Life in the Church is like being in a great ship.

Every ship needs a sail and a rudder. The sail catches the wind. The rudder guides the ship to its final destination across a vast ocean. Without the rudder, the ship gets off course, and no matter how fair a wind we catch, we end up missing our port and risk crashing on the rocky shore. Without the sail we cannot catch the wind, and no matter how much we move the rudder, we go nowhere. The sail catches the wind, which is the power of God's love in the Holy Spirit. The rudder is God's truth. We need both to safely navigate the oceans of life.

The wind of the Spirit empowers us. We must learn to skillfully raise the sails of our spiritual lives to catch the wind. The wind propels us, but in the hands of a skilled sailor, a well-raised sail can itself direct the ship on its course. But for most of us, we also need a rudder. The rudder is the revealed truth of God that leads us safely to port. God's truth is called *orthodoxy*, or right belief, or right praise of God.

Without the rudder of true orthodoxy, many well-meaning charismatic Christians have ended up crashing on the rocks of personal and communal error regarding faith and morality. Sometimes their lives and movements are left as wrecks on the rocky shores.

Without the well-raised sail to really catch the charismatic gifts and fruit of the Holy Spirit, professional religious leaders get nowhere. They might know well how to operate the rudder of orthodoxy and truth regarding faith and morality, but they lack the real power of the spirit of God. Religion that lacks the power of the Holy Spirit knows the form of godliness without really knowing the power of God.

But raising the sail takes skill. It takes practice. You learn it from an experienced sailor, who has personally known the great Sailor. This keeps us from making too many costly mistakes, the kinds that might tempt us to give up sailing altogether.

Some try to swim the great oceans without being on the ship at all. Many of them drown, despite being expert swimmers. We all need the ship of the Church. But for the Church to fulfill her real role, she needs a sail to catch the Spirit and the rudder of truth to guide her safely home.

Naked Wrestling and Poverty

Gospel poverty enriches all who embrace it. It prunes what is not fruitful, so that we might bear abundant spiritual fruit. We renounce all to gain everything.

The Early Church Fathers liken Gospel poverty and simplicity to wrestlers.

Wrestlers in those days wrestled naked so as to give their opponents no loose clothing to grab in order to defeat them. They also covered their bodies with oil to make themselves too slippery for their opponents to take hold of them.

Likewise, in the spiritual life we divest ourselves of the outer clothing of all our possessions and our need to possess so the devil cannot grab us. We are also anointed with the Holy Spirit, given through both the waters of Baptism and the oil of chrism at both Baptism and Confirmation, so that if the devil grabs us, we are too slippery to hold!

Another comparison is the traveler. We travel light so we are not weighed down by concerns that come with excess baggage.

This is also true of the spiritual life. The more we have, the more we must be concerned with, and the more we must maintain and defend. This makes us anxious, upset, and unable to focus on the more important things of the Gospel. It also causes us to be defensive in a way that does not befit a minister of the Gospel of Jesus Christ.

What do we really need on a journey? We must differentiate between what we need and what we want. Habitually indulging our wants may steal from and eventually even kill the needy. It also kills us. We often think we need things we only want. Then we are addicted and deluded. We are often possessed by our possessions and consumed by what we consume. Instead of using creation as a gift from God, we misuse and abuse it, making it an obstacle to our journey to God.

When we free ourselves of the attraction and distraction of unnecessary possessions, we can encounter the naked spirit of God with a naked soul. We can give ourselves to him freely without encumbrance. This is the gift of Gospel poverty.

Are you sometimes pulled away from God by excess possessions? Is there anything in your life that you find yourself unable to give to him?

The Train Track and Obedience

A train track used to run next to the farm where I lived in Indiana. When the trains came by a couple of times a day, they shattered the usual quiet of the farm. I was always amazed at the sheer power of those engines that were able to pull freight trains more than a mile long behind them. And I was grateful that the tracks guided the trains.

Obedience is the way to real freedom. It is the way to deeper joy and peace. It is rooted in love.

Obedience is like a train and a track. The train might have great power, but without the track it cannot reach its destination. At best it will simply grind away deeper and deeper into the track bed and go nowhere. But usually it ends up mangled in a complete train wreck.

The train is like the power of the Spirit. The track is the guidance of God through the Church and our spiritual fathers or mothers. Without the power of the Spirit, we just sit on the track and go nowhere. But without the guidance of the track, we grind ourselves around and around into the ground of the same old issues and problems; we cannot reach our destination, and ultimately we careen into destruction.

Obedience does not imprison us. It liberates us! Obedience is the truest way to freedom. It restrains our old selves. But it does so in order that the new self can truly rise up and live in Christ. Obedience helps us discover who we really are.

To be obedient means to listen. It means daring to hear what God is saying to us, directly through the spirit of God as well as through others. Obedience teaches us to love and respect God, and to love and respect others. It also acts promptly. If all we do is listen without acting, we deceive ourselves. Through obedience we listen to God and then act with eager promptness.

Obedience teaches us love and joy. It is filled with a spirit that is light. If we listen or act while grumbling or complaining, we are not really obedient. We are merely compliant. There is a big difference between obedience and compliance. Real obedience is joyful and prompt. It gives life to the one who obeys.

If we are obedient to God, we must also be obedient to other people. This is especially true regarding God's experienced and wise leaders in the Church, monastic communities, and valid ministries. We are even called to obey civil authority when it is in communion with God and the Church. In monasteries we are obedient to spiritual fathers and mothers and those who are delegated to help us. In families we are obedient to God and to parents. We must all be obedient to God.

We are wise to seek out spiritual fathers or mothers who act as elders to help us to cultivate a spirit of willing obedience. They accompany us and point out the pitfalls that they and others have encountered on the path. They also walk ahead of us to lead us on our way.

We are obedient to leaders when we agree with them and when we don't, and to those whom we personally like and those we don't. As long as they direct according to the teaching of the Church and the rules of our monasteries or ministries, we obey them.

Real monastic obedience is rarely tested in the big things such as the evangelical counsels of poverty, chastity, and obedience. We discover the big ego attachments and disobedience in the little things. In the monastery, we say we must learn how to "grow a green bean for God." This means that a leader or work supervisor may ask us to grow a green bean in a way different from what we would choose to do on our own. It is at these times that we are tested in our vocations. Someone may also ask us to grow a green bean in a way we personally like or in a way that bristles or offends us. But if a person is acting according to the teaching of the Church and the monastery, and it still gets the job done, we obey. We learn to find the voice of God in those times, teaching us the way of the Cross that leads to real resurrection. Because of this we can be obedient with great joy.

The old monastic story about planting cabbages upside down when commanded to do so by an elder illustrates obedience. The monk who did so saw a plentiful crop! The same is true of planting a twig and watering it when commanded by the elder. It came to life and bore much fruit. Such stories seem beyond belief, but they hold a deeper truth. Obedience, even when we do not understand it—maybe *especially* when we do not understand it—bears spiritual fruit.

This is easy to agree with when reading a spiritual treatise or book. It is much harder to practice in real life.

Our obedience to God, however, can be measured by how we obey our leaders when we do not like them or agree with them, but they still act in accordance with the Church, our community, or our ministry. They aren't abusing us. We just do not like or agree with them.

We obey in charity so that their leadership is not an undue burden for them. But we obey our leaders, not just for them, but for God who established their leadership and works through them for us. When we obey God's leaders, we obey God. We also obey because in the long run it is actually better for us. That is because God loves us more than we even love ourselves.

Obedience to God that is not mediated through experienced leaders can be an illusion that can further degenerate into complete delusion. Without a leader to flesh things out, we can often become obedient merely to ourselves or even to deceptive spirits. When we obey what we think is God's inner voice, determined by our own discernment alone, we can easily fall into the trap of making God according to our image rather than allowing him to mold us into his image and likeness. Mediated authority puts feet to our feelings and fleshes out our desire to obey God in action. Thinking we are obedient to God without action, we can fall into the deception of the adversary who wants us to serve only ourselves, or even to serve him, the author of lies.

Have the strength and drive of a train, but always put your train on a track. Then you will reach your spiritual destination in Christ.

Chastity and Love with Jesus

Chastity is a thing of great beauty. It is pure, unsoiled, and clean. Chastity is not about what we give up but rather what we gain.

Chastity is not about giving up human relationships but rather gaining right ones through an intimate and personal love relationship with Jesus. It is not only about finding the right relationships; it is also about doing right relationships in the right way. Be it chaste celibacy or marriage, chastity enriches them both. Chastity gracefully separates us from all in order to be united with all. In chastity God fulfills our need to be loved.

Chastity is like a clear, clean window through which the Son may brightly shine. The window does not obstruct the rays of the Son. It does not deform them. It does not color them. Chastity is a window for the Son.

Chastity is almost completely overlooked in today's Western culture of promiscuity. To embrace it is radically countercultural and prophetic. It takes courage and great faith.

Our celibate or conjugal chastity on earth and our chastity in our love with Jesus mystically reflect and strengthen one another. The two are intimately interconnected. This is mystical and can only be correctly practiced in the Spirit.

Chastity in Jesus is pure of heart and of single mind, focused in our affections of the heart and inviolate in the body. The same is true on earth. Chastity keeps our hearts pure, our minds single, the emotions of our hearts focused, and our bodies pure.

If we enter into the spiritual unchastity of fornication or adultery, we cannot know whose child we bear. If we are chaste with Jesus, all our spiritual children clearly and inviolately bear his name. They are the fruit of our chaste relationship with him.

On earth some scientists have said that a woman absorbs and stores the DNA of every person with whom she has intimate sexual relations. The same is true spiritually. Our spiritual DNA absorbs and stores the spirits with whom we have intimate relations. If our relations are with Jesus Christ alone, then we absorb him and him alone. And our offspring are purely his.

The stages of our spousal relations on earth also reflect the stages of our spiritual life in Christ as our Lover. Dialogue reflects the need for solid objective teaching and the development of doctrine. Marital consummation reflects the more enthusiastic and charismatic dimensions of our spiritual union with Christ that are beyond objective knowledge. Pregnancy and birth reflect how we bear the fruit of the Spirit in the active life of contemplation and virtuous living that overflow into evangelization of helping birth new Christians. And daily family life represents the day-in and day-out challenges of raising new Christian disciples in the Church.

Chastity is much more than simply restricting our natural impulses for sex. It is a mystical reality that enlivens our celibacy, marriage, and our spiritual life in Christ.

The Monk and the Monastery

A monk sees himself as linked to all others because he sees himself in all others. A monk is a person on fire with love for God, one who has given up all and separated himself from all in order to know intense mystical union with the Creator of all.

A monk is like a person from another world. The things of this world become tasteless to a monastic. Yet in this holy detachment the monk comes to truly experience the created world with a heightened awareness and heavenly appreciation that comes from knowing the Creator of the world.

The monk is one who turns only to heavenly realms and so becomes effective on earth. The monk seeks to be a divine creature from another world, and so comes to bring the reconciliation of Jesus to this world.

The monk seeks to be a pilgrim and a stranger, and so is everywhere at home.

Likewise, the monastery should be a dwelling from another world. The elements of the secular city should be totally absent in the city of God. Yet the monastery should be a place of true artistic beauty and environmental balance, reflecting as a mirror on the earth the heavenly beauty and balance of the divine Artist.

The monastery should be a place of keen environmental beauty and sensitivity, where the delicate and fragile dimensions of all creation are properly experienced, appreciated, and savored, so as to lead the solitary community of monks to the constant praise of God.

Let the monastery be a place of silence, so that the great dynamic reality of the living Word of God will always be heard and proclaimed there. Let it be a place of environmental asceticism so as to foster a heightened aware-ness of the delicate aesthetic beauties of the created world.

Yes, let the monastery be like a dwelling from another world, and it will increase sensitivity to the created beauty of all the world and so help lead all creation to God.

There is a universal monasticism made up of all monas-tics and all monasteries. St. Bonaventure, in the wisdom of his last years, called this universal monasticism a seraphic, or angelic, order. He contrasted it to the organized orders to which he belonged as a Franciscan and to which he some-times gave the name "seraphic" in his earlier years. It com-prises all orders, unites all orders, and surpasses all orders.

It is also for all states of life. While recognizing the primacy of the celibate monastic call, St. John Chrysostom said that anyone—married, single, or celibate—who knows Jesus personally and lives the Gospel without compromise is rightly a monk. Such a universal monasticism knows no human boundaries.

It is to this universal order that I wish to belong. It is to this universal monasticism that I am grateful to belong and that I humbly receive and boldly pass on to others.

Meeting the Magi

They came from the religions of the Near East. They came in search of the newborn king. They came not by reading scripture or studying under Jewish teachers but by following a star. The Magi serve as a good example for us.

Many are nervous about the interfaith work of the Church. They are rightly concerned about slipping into a syncretic universalism that ignores the uniqueness of Christ and Christianity. Yet this work is vital in a world where religions must learn not only to coexist but also to cooperate in bringing religious freedom and tolerance for any faith engaged in building a better and more peaceful world. Jesus himself confirmed the good in all religions. He completes them and surpasses them all.

The Magi were not Jewish, much less orthodox Jews! Yet they had been alerted to the birth of Jesus as a newborn king, not by the scriptures or teachers of God's Chosen People, but by observing the stars and the wisdom of their own faith.

Likewise, many non-Christians are led to Jesus Christ by the faithful practice of their own religion. Through what we Catholic Christians call natural revelation, they search for the good, the holy, and the true to satisfy the spiritual longings common to all humanity. Natural revelation is not perfect or infallible, but it does point the discerning seeker in the direction of God and his Son, Jesus Christ.

The Magi were not driven away from the Holy Family and Jesus. They were welcomed. They presented the Holy Family and Jesus with worship and precious gifts. Gold, frankincense, and myrrh were richly significant and necessary to fund the Holy Family during their sojourn in Egypt.

The Magi were sincere practitioners of their beliefs. Herod, however, typifies insincere religious adherents of any faith. Do we welcome or rebuff those of other faiths who sincerely seek the way, truth, and life that only comes in Jesus? Jesus is the way, the truth, and the life. What is this way, this truth, and this life? It is not limited to the way of correct doctrine; it encompasses the way of paradox and mystery. Paradoxes often speak deeper truths for which every humble human heart seeks. They defy the mind but enlighten the spirit and soul. They also energize the body.

Other great religious founders and leaders point to this way, truth, and life. They do so with greater or lesser degrees of accuracy. World religions are part of natural revelation. They all have wonderful mystics and masters who teach objective faith and morality, and meditation and prayer to help achieve communion and mystery. But they only point the way. They are not fully the way, the truth, and the life.

Only the Jewish faith reveals the way with accuracy, but without Christ it is still incomplete. Judaism is more than just natural revelation. The Jewish scriptures bring supernatural revelation, and Jesus completes them all.

Only Jesus incarnates this reality fully. He is the Word made flesh. Like others, he teaches it with words to disciples, and he humbly points to God his Father as the source. But Jesus does more than point to the way, truth, and life; he incarnates it. Jesus *is* the way, truth, and life!

Jesus is God in man, life in death, glory in humiliation, power in weakness. He is wealth in poverty, freedom in obedience. He is the Word in silence, and communion in solitude. He is the Paradox of paradoxes, the Mystery of mysteries, the King of kings, and the Lord of lords.

Some teach a syncretic universalism that ignores the uniqueness of Jesus and the incompleteness of other religions. Others teach a fulfillment that ignores the truth of other faiths. Only Jesus confirms and completes in a way that fulfills and surpasses all.

He does so without arrogance and pride. He simply is. He simply lives as the Word that confirms and completes all true teachings and words.

Are you willing to do the same?

The Oil Painting and the Line Drawing

The difference between theology and mystical experience is like the difference between a line drawing and a rich oil painting. It's the difference between theology *about* Jesus and a personal encounter *with* Jesus.

Jesus is like a rich oil painting. The subtle colors and hues of his beautiful face are brought through sacred scripture, apostolic tradition, and the teaching authority of the Church that includes mystics and theologians alike. His face is painted through the mysteries of the liturgy, the sacraments, and the witness of the saints.

Theology alone is like a line drawing. The lines might be more or less in the right place, but the rich colors and subtle hues of the oil painting are not there. These must come from personal encounter, from mystical experience.

When I became a Catholic I was stunned at the love for Jesus I found in the Church. I had always heard that Catholics love Mary or other saints more than Jesus. But it isn't my experience.

I came into the Church through the Franciscan doorway. (St. Francis's personal encounter with Jesus was so radical that he was often called "another Christ.") The friars I met were wonderful. My spiritual father was a Catholic charismatic who was conversant in things Catholic and non-Catholic. His love for Jesus was palpable.

In the non-Catholic world I heard a lot of talk about Jesus. There was ample doctrine and theology about Jesus, and a lot of talk about a personal love relationship with Jesus Christ. But I found that very few had experienced the incarnate person of Jesus Christ. He often remained only an idea or a theology at best. Consequently, the theology fell short.

Jesus remained a word in a book. It was very much an "Old Testament" experience, even though the theology and law it championed were claiming to flow from a New Testament based on a real relationship with Jesus Christ.

For me, discovering the lives and writings of the saints of the Catholic tradition was like moving from a line drawing of Jesus to a rich oil painting. A line drawing gets the outer lines correctly, but without the subtle colors and rich hues of an oil painting, it fails to capture a living being. With a personal encounter with Jesus Christ, you move beyond a mere line drawing to a rich oil painting where his eyes pierce into the depths of your soul. They change you forever as you literally fall through them into his spirit and soul.

For me, all that came before was merely a line drawing. The Christian world outside Catholic tradition wasn't necessarily wrong, but the living subtlety and mystery of Jesus was absent. It was very black and white. It was all about the theology of Jesus and the scriptures written about Jesus. But somehow it lacked an actual experience that could empower folks to become more and more like Jesus.

Of course, there are exceptions to this generalization, and there are great saints from the Protestant and evangelical worlds. But as a movement, evangelicalism remained for me like eating oatmeal without brown sugar or cinnamon. It lacked the flavor of the mystical and incarnate person of Jesus Christ.

And, too, there are many Catholic leaders and members who have yet to really enter into that personal encounter with Jesus Christ. For them, Jesus is still a line drawing as well.

Are we allowing Jesus to take us from line drawings to rich oil paintings? Are we allowing him to bring color and subtle beauty into our lives?

Integration and the Cord

I am a Catholic Christian who came into the Church through Franciscan and monastic doors. I am also a musician who has seen the move of acoustic to electric, and the advent of synthesized sound. Meditating on the Franciscan cord taught me about integration.

I live in an integrated monastic community, but we are not a synthesized community. There is a difference.

Integration is like two or three cords being woven together to form a rope. In the weaving process the distinct character of each cord is retained, but they work together to form something bigger and stronger.

Synthesis is the disintegration of the uniqueness of each individual part to form something brand new. It distorts one sound to blend it with another to appear as if it is something that it is not, such as synthesized strings or voices. This is fine for live performance, where it is often impractical to have extra musicians. It is also legitimate as a real sound unto itself. But it is not ordinarily good to appear to be something that you are not.

The Brothers and Sisters of Charity are integrated, meaning that we take various unique aspects of Christian, Catholic, and monastic Franciscan life and interweave them to form something new. Nevertheless, what we build on is very surely and very perceivably the apostolic and religious traditions of our Christian past.

Integration and Community

Integration is a key expression of our community's primary charism of love. Integration comes from the personal encounter with Jesus on the Cross. On the Cross, through his outstretched arms of love, Jesus reconciles the height of heaven and the depths of the earth, the far left and the far right of the earth. The things that contradict one another in the world may now complement one another in Christ. This brings much integrated diversity as long as all is centered squarely on the Cross of Jesus, where God's love for all is manifested perfectly.

Integration also comes from a realization of the healthy interdependence shared by all the members of the Church, all peoples of the world, and all creatures of creation. This attitude causes us to become truly *catholic*, or universal and full, as we seek to receive all God's gifts that come to us through creation, the human race, and the Church, and to find our place in healthy relationship to each. Because of this, the scope of the community is international and universal.

The Brothers and Sisters of Charity integrate various aspects of Christian tradition into a manifest, living whole, to more effectively share the holistic beauty of this balanced tradition with others. As such, our community integrates all religions from a uniquely Christian base, all Christian faiths from a uniquely Catholic base, and all religious and monastic traditions from a uniquely Franciscan base. Thus we are wholly ecumenical and integrated from an intentionally Franciscan, Catholic foundation.

We also bring together apparent contradictions into complements on other levels. We intentionally integrate charismatic and contemplative spiritualities. We integrate liturgical and spontaneous prayer. We integrate our call to solitude with our call to community. We integrate our primary call to contemplative community with our call to overflow into apostolic action through individual and community ministry and service.

Within the structure of the community itself, we integrate our specific and unique calls to live in the single, celibate, or married states into a balanced and living whole. Thus there are proper integrations between male and female single, celibate, and married members in our community. Likewise, we integrate the clerical and lay, the monastic and secular, states in our community. As such, we build on the monastic tradition that sees the community itself as a quasi-church, and we look prophetically toward the future as a microcosm and possible prototype of the Church.

Because of this, members of our community draw inspiration from the entire monastic tradition. Knowing that the word *monk* means "alone," we follow the hermetical example of the Desert Fathers and Mothers of Egypt, especially St. Anthony of the Desert. But acknowledging that we do this as brothers and sisters in community, we also draw inspiration from the cenobitic tradition established by St. Pachomius. We emulate the moderation and stability of St. Benedict's Rule, as well as the emphasis on brotherly love in the common life found in the rule of St. Augustine. As a semi- or socio-eremitical community, we also find inspiration in the original Carmelite rule. The constitutions and leaders of the many semi-eremitical reforms of the eleventh century provide us powerful examples to follow, especially St. Bruno, who founded the Carthusians (whom I almost joined in England), and the Camaldolese of St. Romuald, with whom the Franciscans share so much history. The integrated double monasteries of the Celtic monks guide our integrations between single, celibate, and married members, living together in appropriate expressions in our monastic village.

We also recognize and emulate the hermits, pilgrims, and itinerant preachers of the penitential movement, from which the whole Franciscan family was born. That move of the Spirit gave birth not only to the mendicant friars of the First Order and the contemplative sisters of the Second Order, but also to the rich and diverse congregations of brothers and sisters of the Third Order Regular and Secular of St. Francis, or the Brothers and Sisters of Penance.

Because of our Franciscan base, we observe the Holy Gospel of our Lord Jesus Christ after the example of St. Francis and St. Clare of Assisi. We first seek to understand and live the beautiful tradition of contemplation of heart that is traceable back to the holy lady, St. Clare. We then seek to understand and live by the light of the simple and wise friar St. Anthony of Padua. We seek to understand and live the freedom of our royal Lady Poverty, which is traceable in heart and mind back to our little brother and holy father, St. Francis. The rules and writings of Francis and Clare serve as important sources of inspiration for our lives as Brothers and Sisters of Charity.

Still, we recognize and are inspired by the various non-Catholic movements that so strongly emphasize intense alternative approaches to family-oriented Christian community, such as the Mennonites of Menno Simons, the Amish of Jakob Ammann, and the Quakers of George Fox.

In addition, the ashrams, or communities of the non-Christian religions of the East, have much to teach us regarding lifestyle and human meditation. Of course, we integrate these practices from our Catholic, Christian, Franciscan base, retaining orthodox doctrine, integrity of sacraments, and obedience to the authorities over us, both as individuals and as a community.

Finally, at the root and center of all that we are on earth, we seek the divine love of Jesus Christ, our Lover and our Lord, who leads us to the Father under the guidance of the

Holy Spirit and the gospels, which serve as our primary rule of life.

Promises of the Heart

In our community we profess the three traditional evangelical counsels of consecrated life. These form the heart of our way of life.

Poverty: To live a life of apostolic poverty so others might know the wealth of the King of kings.

Chastity: To live a life of chastity so others might be wed to the divine Lover.

Obedience: To live a life as bondservants to the King in obedience so others might know the freedom of coheirs to his kingdom and the divine authority of him who first humanly obeyed.

In addition to these three primary covenants, we may also profess the following covenants:

Substantial Silence: To live life with an attitude of humble silence so that others might hear the living Word of the Gospel of Jesus Christ.

Substantial Solitude: To live a life of substantial solitude so others might come to know the presence of the constant Companion.

Prayer: To live a life of contemplative prayer so others might experience the divine action of Jesus' love in their lives.

Penance: To live a life of daily self-denial and conversion so others might turn daily to the comfort of the spirit of Christ in their lives.

The Master Musician

Life with Jesus and in the Church is like music.

God creates with music, for all sound and light is harmonious waves perceived by ears and eyes. All seen and unseen physical dimensions are waves vibrating to make harmony and music from God. Sin brings discord in every dimension. It keeps the dimensions from vibrating together.

The Church is the harp of God, and each of us is a string on the harp. Each string is unique and has its own note to play. Our strings must be tuned to make music with others.

Jesus is the master musician. He is the composer and the conductor. He is also the music. He is the Note behind all notes, and the Sound behind all sounds. He is also the space and silence between the notes where the deeper music of God is often best found.

Jesus is the master musician, and we are his instruments.

We are like guitars to be played by God. Jesus makes us into his instrument.

A guitar is made by cutting down a tree. Jesus chooses only the best trees and the best wood. But the tree must be brought down to get at the best wood. Only then can it become a beautiful instrument for God.

This is like embracing the Cross at the very beginning of our spiritual lives in Christ. We are chosen to be brought down, not because we are bad but because we are good, maybe even the best. But we must allow him to bring us down right at the base of our lives. This is radical, and it must be complete. But this is not the end. It is only the beginning.

Next, the wood is cut into small pieces, dried, and aged. It takes time and patience.

After that, the necessary pieces are fashioned. They are assembled, glued, and held into place by a soft brace. These are the various traditional spiritual disciplines that reshape us after his likeness, by allowing his strong yet tender touch.

Then the wood is sanded and varnished repeatedly. We might still have rough edges, still lack strength. But the light and delicate varnish protects and allows the wood to sing each tone. This is like what occurs in our life with others in community. We are buffed, shined, and strengthened by the Spirit. This makes us stronger and more beautiful. It protects us and allows the tones of God to sing in our lives.

Then we are strung. The strings must be neither too tight nor too loose. This is like the creative tension in our spiritual life in Christ and the Church. Too tight, and we snap. Too loose, and we make no music at all.

Lastly, we remember that the more we are played by Jesus, the more we conform to his touch. A good guitar actually conforms to the touch and style of the one who plays it the most. One that is played frequently often resonates best.

Playing the Guitar

To properly play the guitar we must study under a good teacher, and we must practice. I had great teachers in my formative years. I also practiced almost constantly. I remember practicing until my fingers bled. Slowly my fingers built up callouses. Then they cracked and bled some more. Eventually they became soft and pliable callouses that could endure playing steel or nylon strings.

I also practiced scales. Scales aren't particularly pleasant to listen to, and they are hard to learn. But they are absolutely necessary. Without them you cannot play any music with ease.

I learned various styles. I played folk, rock, country, a bit of jazz, and even some classical music. Only then did I develop the freedom to play any style. I also learned to play other people's music. I practiced the music of those I admired. I copied their technique and tone. But in time something surprising happened. My own music began to emerge as something completely unique from anyone else's.

The same is true with singing and songwriting. I studied and slavishly rehearsed others' success. Only after decades did my own music and my own voice emerge.

Are you beginning to realize your own music, your own song?

Musical Periods and the Church

There are different periods in music. They can represent different periods in Church history and different spiritualities that have developed through time and space into the present.

The primitive music of Eastern and Western chant represents the first scriptural period of the Church. It is almost primal but speaks to a deep place in the human spirit and soul. It defies modern keys through the use of modes, and in some ways it is more advanced and expressive than modern music.

Polyphony is the interplay of multiple melodies in a most pleasant way. It predates modern harmony and represents the patristic and early monastic period. It includes what modern music would call brief dissonance but brings an interplay and counterpoint that makes music interesting and expressive.

Classical music is the first fruit of modern harmony. It represents a brilliance and spirituality that is based on perfect math, counterpoint, and resolution. It is seen in the Scholastic period in the West and Byzantine period in the East. It is beautiful and interesting, but sometimes it is too logical and can feel sterile. Human experience defies such strict categorization. So does God.

The sterility of classical music is followed by a correction in the Romantic music period. Using much of the same ideas as classical, the Romantic music seeks to rediscover the human heart. But it can sometimes be melodramatic or syrupy. It represents the devotional period of the West.

Impressionistic music seeks to rediscover the harmony that defies strict math and resolution. It takes seemingly dissonant notes played in a chromatic succession that brings out a certain beauty as seen in nature. It reminds us that the beauty of God is sometimes beyond human logic and is best expressed in mystery.

Musical minimalism takes rapidly repeating notes and creates a meditational state when viewed beyond the individual notes to the overarching ebbs and flows of the whole. Like driving on a highway, we do not obsessively look at each repeating line but at the progressive lines as a whole, to keep the car straight without getting nervous and upset. This is much like the contemplative in the modern city.

The Symphony

A symphony is a piece of music written for a full orchestra. It is written by a living human composer and recorded in notes on a page. To play the notes correctly, we must understand the technology of written music. But we must also understand the spirit of the composer; otherwise, the notes remain as they are on the page—technically correct but spiritless. That is how dead music is made.

Liturgy is like music in this way. Jesus is the composer. Liturgy and rubrics are the sheet music. We must understand the principles of liturgy in order to pray it properly. But we must also understand the spirit of the Composer. Without the Spirit, liturgy remains dead actions and words. The liturgy holds the spirit of the Composer, but prayer and real conversion must unlock it. Without prayer and personal conversion, liturgy remains just vainly repeated words and gestures.

This is also true with the sacraments. Sacraments contain the grace they signify and bring it about. They symbolize faith, and they confirm and strengthen faith. Sacraments hold the explosive power of God within. They affect that power in ways beyond our ability to know consciously. The sacraments are mysteries. But they must also be approached with faith to be fully experienced on the conscious level. They simply wait to be fully unlocked.

The Orchestra

An orchestra meets in many configurations to play various kinds of music. It is big, and it creates a big sound. Each player is an expert in his or her instrument and highly familiar with the composers who have written music for that instrument. The conductor knows each instrument, player, and composer in order to call forth the greatest performances from the orchestra.

The Church is like an orchestra.

An orchestra must have a conductor, sections of instruments, and section leaders; it plays sheet music. In the Church, Jesus is the conductor. In his physical absence on earth, the bishop of Rome is his vicar and conducts in his name. Sections are the dioceses, and the bishops are section leaders.

The full symphony orchestra plays the bigger pieces. This is like the Eucharist, the Divine Liturgy or Mass. It is the source and summit of our life together in Christ. It is the fullest expression of our faith.

The chamber orchestra plays the smaller and more intimate pieces, but it still functions like the full symphony orchestra. This represents formal communities of the Church, praying the Divine Office by dioceses and parishes, or monastics and communities of consecrated life or ministries.

The string quartet plays intricate pieces from sheet music but does not have a conductor. It is led by one of the players. This represents smaller monasteries and communities of consecrated life or ministries.

Folk groups do not usually play sheet music. They represent the less formal spiritual movements of the Church. They are great vehicles for informal prophetic teaching. They are conducted directly by the Holy Spirit, though the Spirit might use one particular leader whom the group naturally follows. They are the popular movements of the Church.

Rock groups play with raw power and emotion. They represent the cry of a fallen world and the evangelization of a fallen culture to reach a culture where it is, and lead it back to Christ.

The jazz group is composed of highly trained musicians who are experts at improvisation. Their virtuosity is famous. These represent those skilled in the things of the Holy Spirit and spontaneous prayer. They can read classical music or improvise in a way that lifts us to heaven.

Meditational music represents the contemplative reality of Jesus. He is the One Note that holds all notes and all sounds in One Sound. He is also the music in the space between the notes.

The soloist has a place in all these groups. Even the full symphony orchestra has room for soloists, and even some improvisation. These are the itinerant hermits and preachers who fulfill a prophetic role in the context of the greater Church.

The full integration of one or more of the above expressions is a growing trend in orchestral music. When done rightly it is an awe-filled experience for player and listener alike. This can also be seen in the Church, when formal and informal work together in prayer and ministry. It is rare. But when it occurs, it calls forth awe in the Spirit that is unsurpassed by any one expression alone.

In this extended analogy, we know that Jesus is the master musician. Jesus is the luthier—the guitar maker—and we are the instruments. Jesus is the composer and the conductor. We are the orchestra. And the music is the full harmony of the creation of God with God himself.

Is Jesus making music from the discord in your life?

PART FOUR

The Future Lies before Us

Universal Signs

It is important to bring the miracle of Jesus back into mundane life. We must find the miracle *in* the mundane before we can bring miracles *to* the mundane. We must be faithful in the ordinary things of life before we can expect to accomplish anything extraordinary for Jesus.

This is true especially at Mass. We participate firsthand in sacramental incarnation, bringing the miracle of the first Incarnation of Jesus into the here and now. The Cross, where he poured out his entire life for you and me personally, is brought into the present at each Eucharist. The wonder of the Resurrection is brought to us as a personal experience in each liturgy. Then we go forward to the greatest altar call that can be given. We receive the living Body and Blood of Christ. After this miracle we proceed back to the same place in the pew or choir stall where we started.

And it continues as we return to our homes, our workplaces, to live with loved ones and coworkers. We must bring the extraordinary back into the ordinary things of our daily lives right where we are. The Mass never ends—it must be lived!

After Mass, where is this immediately tested? In the parking lot!

Once, I had just finished singing and sharing at Mass, and I went to leave the church. Apparently some guy did not like the way I was driving. He was all red-faced, and he was screaming at me. I had my windows up, so I couldn't hear him, but I knew what he was saying! Then he flipped me the universal sign! I couldn't believe it. Right after we had both presumably received Jesus in Holy Communion together.

At first I noticed the most unchristian things rising up in my thoughts, such as "I've been driving longer than you've been alive," and so forth. Then it started to spread to my emotions. It did not feel Christlike. So I stopped, breathed in the spirit of Jesus, and breathed out my old self that so easily gets offended by such things. Then I began to feel great love for this person.

So I decided to give him a universal sign—the Sign of the Cross! And I smiled at him. He didn't know what to do. I just loved him.

What kind of universal signs are we sharing regularly in our lives?

Dreams and Sister Death

I was recently in the hospital. I was so ill that thoughts hurt, and words were impossible. All I could do was moan unintelligible sounds so soft that they were audible only to me. Yet the Word of God in those words was completely understandable in a way beyond objective thought. His thought was clear.

I felt my spirit passing over to the other side, to God. All on earth seemed unimportant. All that I had ever accomplished seemed unimportant in the scope of what I was beginning to experience. This experience is related to some of my dreams.

I have had only two dreams of my spiritual father. Both were not long after his death. In the first, he was in the small library of our first monastery. He was pointing toward the big books of theology and canon law. He lifted his index finger and waved it, as if to say, "These are not important up here." I love to study, so this meant that study is good on earth, but in heaven all eternal knowledge simply *is*. All other knowledge is passed away.

In the second dream, he was in a vast sanctuary standing at an altar with innumerable altars in God. The gist was that he was at the edge, close to the nave, so he was still new in the eternal.

Now, I have sometimes struggled with the call to be a priest, though I am far too old for that to be a possibility now. A cardinal friend of mine once said that a man could only be effective in the Catholic Church if he were a priest. Though that is still largely true, it so turned me off that I elected not to go that way. Instead, I chose the way of non-clerical monastics.

In the dream my spiritual father looked at me as if to say, "You can come join me." Then he looked past me, and there were many priests and religious filing up to the sanctuary, as if he were saying, "Your ministry is bringing many priests and religious into their vocations and leading them to heaven." He then looked back at me as if to say, "You still have work to do on earth." So I have stayed a bit longer. But I am ready to go.

Sickness and Death

I have recently faced a long string of serious illnesses. I knew that God was calling me to be ready to die. When and whether that will occur in body or in spirit I cannot say. But my old self must die in a major way. Kindness and love are all that matter. It is time to let younger or at least wiser men handle the more objective part of the Church and community. As St. Francis said, "I've done my part. May Christ teach you yours."

At the beginning of my vocation and ministry, God also gave me a few messages. They have proven true. The first message references the book of Ezekiel. "For them you are only a ballad singer with pleasant voice and a clever touch. But when it happens, and it surely will happen, 'they will know that a prophet has been in their midst'" (Ez 33:33, *NASB*). I am no prophet, but as much as I appreciate the success of my music, sometimes all else in my life is overlooked because of its shadow.

The second message was more profound. God told me that I would not enter the Promised Land of the vision he had given me. I will see it from afar but not enter in myself. This is because of my sin. It is because of my ego and pride. It seems that no matter how hard I try to escape them, they manage to reemerge even under the guise of active ministry, objective spirituality, and religion. So for now I do my best to repent, and hope for the future. As with Moses, there are Joshuas. I pray that the Joshuas of my life and ministry will realize the vision that God gave me.

The Lord told me that I would be a catalyst. The catalyst brings together active agents for change. But the catalyst disappears. I pray that as I disappear, the active agents will fulfill the vision God gave me so many decades ago.

We Need Revival

We need revival in the West today. The Western world, once lifted up from paganism and barbarianism, is lapsing back into it in the form of secularism. The Church in the West is bleeding people. Our parishes will soon be empty if we do not turn it around. We are at a Nineveh moment. We can either repent and prosper or not repent and perish. The choice is ours.

Revival means to restore life where it is nearly gone, or even lost. Ezekiel tells us that revival is like raising up dry bones. The dry bones are in the valley. He prophesies over the dry bones, and they are lifted up. Then the spirit of God breathes over them and they become living beings.

We have what we need for revival. The dry bones are all there in the valley of the Church. All we need are prophets to call the revival forth, and those bones will be lifted up and put into the right place. We already have right teaching regarding faith and morality, liturgy and sacraments, Church and God. We only need to lift them up and put them into place once more. But reform is only the beginning. Next we need renewal and revival.

Renewal and revival come from the real breath of the spirit of God. We must open ourselves to a real life in the Spirit. Getting the externals of faith right is not enough. We must be genuinely revived and transformed from the inside out, and from the outside in. It is not enough to have only the form of godliness. We must know the power of God.

But to be revived we must also repent. We must change our minds from the old ways of thinking and doing to a new way. This is true even in the Church, and in our local churches. Just because we have done something one way for years or decades does not mean that it has to be done that way today. If it is not working and does not touch the essence of the Church of the faith, it can be changed. Things can develop.

But here is the reality. Catholics in the West often *want to want* revival. But we do not really *want* revival. Wanting to want revival means that we want things to get better, but we do not really want to change much of anything. We say, "It has been done that way here for years, or decades." How is that working for you?

To want revival means that we are willing to change, update, and develop the things that are not essential to our Catholic faith. They are just the outer forms that are often based more on cultures from the past than on the needs of the present or the future.

Do we really want revival today?

Stepping Out of the Boat

For real revival we must operate in faith. Operating in faith is like stepping out of the boat to walk on water with Jesus.

Ordinarily, water is not made to be walked on. It is made for boating or swimming. But Jesus walks on water, and he invites us to walk on water, too.

When Jesus invited Peter to walk on water, Peter had the courage and the faith to step out of the boat. The boat was safe. It was what Peter knew. To walk on water, Peter had to step out of the boat of his safety zone and away from all he knew to be true. That is what it took to join Jesus on the water.

And Peter did fine for a while—that is, until he took his eyes off Jesus and focused on the waves. He did fine until he focused on the storm. Then he began to sink. He began to sink beneath the waves in the storm. He was certain that he would drown.

But Jesus reached to Peter under the waves, grabbed him by the hand, and pulled him back up to safety. Then Jesus asked Peter, "Why did you doubt? Where is your faith?"

It is the same with you and me. We must be willing to step out of the boats of our safety zones to really walk on water with Jesus. It takes great courage to step out of the lives we know and are comfortable with to follow Christ. We might be stuck in the storm of darkness or sin, but at least we are familiar with it; we feel comfortable in it. Jesus dares us to step out of our boats to walk on water with him.

It takes great faith to walk on water. It means doing something we do not yet understand or comprehend. How can we do it? It is beyond our understanding. But we must take the step out of the boats of our familiarity to fully follow

Christ into a world yet unknown but full of miracles and promise—a world where he is and where he invites us to follow.

Like Peter, we often do well for a while, until we take our eyes off Jesus and focus on the storms and waves of life instead. We focus on the world, not on the kingdom of God. We focus on politics, not on the King of kings. We focus on the mere externals of the faith rather than on faith itself. We see troubles rather than the Comforter, sickness rather than the Healer, and problems rather than the Solution. So we sink. Maybe we do not sink all at once. But we sink nonetheless, one issue at a time, until we fully submerge beneath the waves. And we are often close to drowning.

Jesus reaches to us under the waves of the storms to grab us by our hands and lift us up to safety once more. He lifts us up to walk on water with him once more.

Reach up and grab hold of him. He will not let go of you. You must let go of him. And even then he will search for your hand and hold you tight. Not one is snatched out of his hands.

Let Jesus pull you up from beneath the waves. Walk on water with him once more!

Stones in the Temple

In my integrated monastic community, we merge the various traditions of the past with the present as we build toward the future.

We are the living stones and the spiritual temple of God, built on the foundations of the apostles and the prophets, with Christ Jesus as the cornerstone. All the monastic, religious, and Franciscan traditions of Christianity have been built stone upon stone, course upon course, through almost two thousand years of Christian history. We must build squarely upon the sound traditions of the past if we are to build straight into the future.

However, to simply imitate the past is to go down, rather than go up, in this building process. We must build our stones squarely on all the traditions or stones of the past, but we must build upward into new space if we are to go higher. This involves an element of risk. We build upon the past, but we are called to manifest something new. We are rooted in the past, but our flower must be fresh and new if it is to bring new and fresh beauty into this world.

Therefore, although we are Franciscan in our base, the Lord has given our community a prophetic word to "die to Franciscanism." We must be more Francis, and less Franciscan, and more Jesus than Francis. That was the vision of Francis. Jesus is our primary example, and scripture is our primary rule. In this we are less Francis and more Jesus. Perhaps, though, we are more like Francis and less like Franciscanism. As Francis was called to live the Gospel in his time, so have we been birthed as a fresh and new expression of Gospel living for our time.

As such, Franciscanism is our mother, but we are called to be a child that is unique and new. As the Old Testament was to the New Testament Church, so is Franciscanism to the Brothers and Sisters of Charity. We love our heritage as a child loves its mother. Likewise, we may quote an appeal to the mother to legitimize the child. However, we are not exactly like our mother. We are a child that is unique and new. We must be birthed, mature, and stand as our own person.

Are we ready?

St. Teresa's Prayer:
Christ Has No Body Now But Yours

One of the most beloved songs I have had the pleasure to compose is "St. Teresa's Prayer," or "Christ Has No Body Now But Yours."

This song came as a surprise. A Carmelite friar in Dublin gave it to me written out on a napkin. As so many have said, he was sure that I should put it to music. I did what I usually do: I thanked him, put it in my habit pocket, and went back to my room at the retreat center. I set it on the desk and expected to rest. That didn't happen!

The words drew me mysteriously. I picked up my guitar, played a bit, and the song simply wrote itself with little effort and with little to no reworking. The song has since blessed millions of people all around the world. It was a gift of God's grace greater than my ability could possibly muster.

> Christ has no body now but yours,
> No hands, no feet on earth but yours.
> Yours are the eyes through which he looks
> Compassion on this world.
> Yours are the feet with which he walks
> To do good.
> Yours are the hands with which he blesses
> All the world.
>
> Yours are the hands
> Yours are the feet
> Yours are the eyes
> You are his Body.

Christ has no body now but yours.
No hands, no feet on earth but yours.
Yours are the eyes through which he looks
Compassion on this world.
Christ has no body now on earth but yours.

One moral to this story is that we must always be ready for God's surprises. You never know when God will give you a gift that can bless many others. This gift might come from the most unexpected people, in the most unexpected places and times.

But there is more.

While I sing this song in concert, I have folks hold one another's hands and meditate on the thought that they are holding both the hand of Jesus and the hand of anyone in special need at this time, or anyone with whom we might need reconciliation. The healing tears and reconciliations at these moments are nothing short of miraculous. I am always a bit stunned by such grace at work through my simple little song!

This prayer is a lesson for the whole Church.

We must hold the hand of Jesus in every hand we hold. We must look at everyone with the eyes of Christ and hear the words of Christ in everyone. We must speak only the words of Jesus to everyone. This radically changes the way we touch, look at, hear, or speak to anyone.

This is also the foundation of life in the Church. We are the Body of Christ. We give and receive him in anyone who is part of the entire Church.

It also changes the way we relate to any human being anywhere. All humanity is created in the image of God. When we can see the image of God in even the worst of sinners, we can give Jesus with humility to anyone.

John Michael Talbot is a prolific Catholic singer-songwriter, speaker, and bestselling author who founded an integrated monastic community, the Brothers and Sisters of Charity.

Talbot began performing at age seventeen with his brother Terry in their country folk-rock band Mason Proffit. Since that time, he has recorded more than fifty albums and authored thirty books. He is recognized as one of Catholic music's most popular artists, whose work also is widely held by Christians of other denominations. Talbot's compositions are published in hymnals throughout the world. He received a Dove Award for Worship Album of the Year, *Light Eternal*, with producer Phil Perkins, and is one of nine artists to receive the President's Merit Award (a Grammy) from the National Academy of Recording Arts and Sciences. In 1988 he was named the number-one Christian artist by *Billboard* magazine.

Born into a Methodist family, Talbot explored fundamentalism, Native American religion, Hinduism, Buddhism, Taoism, and the Jesus Movement. That's when he began using his musical talent to express his faith, eventually becoming a pioneer in the contemporary Christian music scene. He studied all Christian denominations, but found that Catholicism spoke to his heart. He was inspired after reading about the life of St. Francis of Assisi and began studying patristics and monasticism at a Franciscan center in Indianapolis, Indiana. He entered the Catholic Church in 1978 and joined the secular Franciscan order. He started a house of prayer called Little Portion, which he later moved to Arkansas. This developed into the Brothers and Sisters of Charity.

Talbot remains the spiritual father and minister general of the Brothers and Sisters of Charity, which also includes St. Clare Monastery in Texas and those who live outside the community. His humanitarian efforts have been recognized by the Mercy Corps with the Mother Teresa Award. He created and was host of *All Things Are Possible with God* on The Church Channel.

Talbot lives as a family monastic with his wife at Little Portion Hermitage in Berryville, Arkansas.

AVE

AVE MARIA PRESS

Founded in 1865, Ave Maria Press,
a ministry of the Congregation of
Holy Cross, is a Catholic publishing
company that serves the spiritual and
formative needs of the Church and its
schools, institutions, and ministers;
Christian individuals and families; and
others seeking spiritual nourishment.

For a complete listing of titles from

Ave Maria Press

Sorin Books

Forest of Peace

Christian Classics

visit www.avemariapress.com

AVE Maria Press
Notre Dame, IN
A Ministry of the United States Province of Holy Cross